SETTLE

A Historic Market Town

David S. Johnson

NORTH CRAVEN HERITAGE TRUST

NORTH
CRAVEN

HERITAGE

www.northcravenheritage.org.uk
http://storiesinstone.org.uk

ISBN 978-1-9160727-4-9
British Library Cataloguing in Publication data
A catalogue record for this book is available from the British Library
Design and Layout: D&AW info@dandaw.com

Front cover:
The actdrop in Victoria Hall showing Market Place c. 1822 (© Victoria Hall)
The coat of arms of Settle Rural District Council (1895 - 1974) (© Nigel
Mussett)

Production of this book was funded by Stories in Stone, a scheme of
conservation and community projects concentrated in the Ingleborough area.
The scheme was developed by the Ingleborough Dales Landscape Partnership,
led by Yorkshire Dales Millennium Trust and supported by the National
Heritage Lottery Fund.

Contents

Acknowledgements

I am grateful to Anne Read MBE for facilitating consent to reproduce archival images from the Museum of North Craven Life collections, to Jean Jelley for granting permission to reproduce archival images from the Horner Collection, to Ann Harding of Victoria Hall for permission to reproduce the front cover image and to Nigel Mussett for specially reproducing the coat of arms of Settle RDC. I owe a debt of gratitude to all those too many to mention who over the years have wittingly or otherwise passed snippets my way or answered my questions. Thanks are also due to the committee and trustees of the North Craven Heritage Trust for logistical support and for believing in the concept, especially John Asher for his sterling efforts, and to the Stories in Stone team for so generously funding production of the book. I make special mention of Rita and the late Phillip Hudson who did so much to further and facilitate research into the history of Settle and North Craven through the now-defunct North Craven Historical Research Group which they founded and ran.

All unattributed colour photographs were taken by the author.

Preface

In my years of involvement in landscape studies one priority has always been to the fore: no focus of detailed study should be viewed in isolation. Why? Simply because nothing exists in a bubble; every place, no matter its size or importance, is what it is partly because of how it has been affected and influenced by its surroundings, by how its inhabitants responded to available opportunities, and by how they adopted, modified and adapted the 'blank cheque' before them. This philosophy prevents me plunging straight into a consideration of Settle the town. First must come Settle's wider landscape, the setting in which the town was founded, grew and blossomed. Thus, the book begins with a look at the physical landscape of the modern parish of Settle – the geological background, tectonic forces that have shaped today's landscape, the topographic detail largely determined by geology, climate and weather, and the botanical veneer which helps make this part of the country such a special place.

After this wider consideration, Chapters 1 and 2 describe the town's origins and growth through the centuries; thenceforth a thematic approach is adopted. The book is aimed at seasoned residents who, hopefully, will find something new; at more recent 'offcumdens' who want to get to know better their adopted town; and at visitors and tourists. This is emphatically not **the** history of Settle: to claim that would be inexcusably arrogant. It is **a** history. It does not set out to be all encompassing; it may not contain everything you the reader hoped for because, inevitably, space restrictions have dictated the number of words, illustrations and pages. What is included here is very much a personal choice.

A long time ago I settled in Upper Ribblesdale in a very cold April having spent fifteen years living and working in tropical Africa. The climate here came as a real shock to me but I was instantly captivated by the landscape, the wide open spaces, the unhurried pace of life, the friendliness of the people ... and the charm of Settle which, it has to be said, was a very different place then from now.

Foreword

His Grace the 12th Duke of Devonshire

I am touched to have been invited to provide a foreword to this book which is so diligently researched and written with a passion for the subject.

Many of you will already know that my family have a long association with North Yorkshire thanks to our home in Bolton Abbey – the place where our children were brought up, and where my wife and I lived for 25 years. Although we are most privileged and happy now to live at Chatsworth in Derbyshire, there is forever a strong pull to North Yorkshire; we love it there, so our visits are as frequent as possible. Our forays 'up Dale' always excite us. We enjoy the stunning scenery, and we notice how towns such as Settle, with its surrounding hamlets and villages, continue to flourish and adapt to life's challenges.

Settle's continuing success should come as no surprise after reading this book. Here is a magnifying glass on a pocket of local history, with which it is my family's good fortune to be connected. In 1748, Charlotte Boyle, a descendant of the formidable Lady Anne Clifford, married William Cavendish, who became the fourth Duke of Devonshire; that marriage brought the manor of Settle into the care of the Devonshire dukedom, where it remains to this day.

Times have changed. The Lord of the Manor is more titular than functional now. I am not called upon, as were my forebears, to mediate in any of the frequent 'disputes about dung', and, I hope, I will never have to back my Steward's (now grandly known as the Estate's Director) damages claim for being called '*a false porky theyf*' as happened in 1777.

Every page holds a gem of the past. And the history related in these pages serves as a pertinent reminder that though things inevitably change, we adapt, we have to survive.

I am sure that you will thoroughly enjoy this book which I heartily recommend.

Chatsworth, April 2020

Introduction

Geology

Seen from afar rather than from within the town, it becomes immediately obvious that Settle (like Giggleswick) nestles in the hollow of higher ground. To the north-west is the bulk of Giggleswick Scar, to the north-east Settle Banks and Warrendale Knotts (maximum height 440m AOD), to the east Castleberg (with or without a final 'h'; 189m AOD) and High Hill (398m AOD), to the south Hunter Bark (315m AOD) and Cleatop Park. Only to the south-west is this ring of hills broken by the broad floodplain of the Ribble in the Bottoms. Settle's topography is shaped, as would be expected, by its underlying geology.

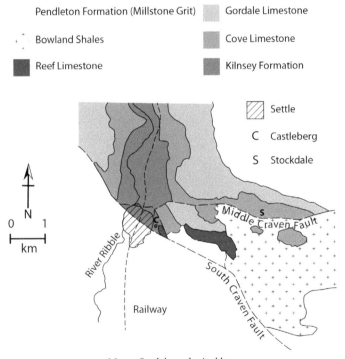

Map 1: Settle's geological base

Settle's geology is made more complex by the presence of tectonic faults (Map 1); it lies within the Craven Fault Zone sandwiched between two major faults. The South Craven Fault (SCF) runs more or less parallel to the A65 from

Ingleton, Clapham and Austwick and follows the line of Buck Haw Brow, cutting through Giggleswick and crossing the Ribble at Queen's Rock then heading south-eastwards again parallel to the A65.

The Ribble in angry mode at Queen's Rock

The Middle Craven Fault (MCF) leaves the SCF in Giggleswick and runs through Stockdale with the Millstone Grits and Bowland Shales of Rye Loaf Hill (547m AOD) on the south side of this Fault and the limestones of Banks and Attermire Scar on the north side. [1]

Warrendale Knotts

The dramatic landscape of Warrendale Knotts is a direct result of tectonic faulting. Limestone outcrops on the north side of the MCF with Bowland Shales and limestone to the south; the vertical downthrow along the fault is about 170m: in other words, the land to the south of the fault has dropped relative to that to the north. The knobbly nature of Warrendale is due to cross-faults between the MCF and SCF: faults are lines of weakness which are opened up by never-ending weathering and erosion. The upland area dominated by High Hill is made up of reef limestones within the Cracoe Limestone Formation, meaning that the rock was formed of compressed corals and algae much as in a present-day tropical coral reef. The area between the two major Craven faults can be termed a shatter zone, geologically a very unstable landscape, but certainly here a dramatic one.

Along the Ribble, downstream from Settle's Penny Bridge all the way to Cow Bridge (Wigglesworth), was a long and narrow, immediately post-glacial lake; eventually the waters carved a way through higher ground draining the lake to leave a flat and often-flooded riverside plain. The most recent manifestation of this lake was Paley's Puddle, long since drained and reclaimed, in the vicinity of Greenfoot and the rugby ground – that is, assuming it ever really existed. A map of Settle, drawn by John Lettsom in 1765 (see Chapter 2), did not include it: surely if it had existed then, he would not have omitted such a significant feature.

Ecology

Settle's varied geology is reflected in its ecology with a range of habitats that support different plant communities. Hunter Bark, the highest part in the south of the parish, and Rye Loaf to the east, are based on Millstone Grit and, where they have not been taken in and 'improved' for stock rearing, they are dominated by upland heathland - heather moor with bilberry. Along Settle's northern boundary, on Banks, Warrendale Knotts and High Hill, the dominant plant community is species-rich calcareous grassland where biodiversity is high with blue-moor grass, common rock-rose, common dog violet and wild thyme being just a few of the flowering species to be seen. Most of Stockdale is either calcareous grassland on the slopes or species-poor pastures in the valley bottom. Between Warrendale and Stockdale the former wetland of Attermire has been altered beyond ecological recognition by centuries of peat cutting.

Peart Crag and Cowpasture Plantation above (old) Anley are semi-natural woodlands with sessile oak and ash; and broadleaved species planted in the last fifteen years or so which are now fighting a battle with the rhododendron and bracken increasingly running wild. Below them is Cleatop Park, recorded as a wood from at least 1612 as 'one great enclosure of woody ground', now owned and managed by the National Park Authority, which is another semi-natural woodland within which invasive and introduced conifers have gradually been removed to restore the wood to its former glory. The 12 hectare Cleatop Wood, between the Park and the A65 and managed by the Woodland Trust, is classified as an 'ancient semi-natural woodland', with the adjacent Stubbing Wood as an 'ancient woodland', dominated by oak and ash with significant numbers of holly, hazel and hawthorn as well as ground species such as dog's mercury, bluebell, primrose and ramsons. Recent plantings, from 2003, comprise sessile oak (40 per cent of the total), ash (20 per cent), alder (10 per cent), silver and downy birch, rowan, hazel, hawthorn and holly.

To the south of Settle, along the Ribble, a very different scene emerges. The rich deposits of lake and river silts were added annually by natural river floods until the plain was enclosed and partially drained in 1779 and again in 1815 to make it suitable for more intensive grazing. Despite these efforts, though, nature is so often wont to return to its natural state with seemingly ever more frequent floods. It is justifiably a Site of Special Scientific Interest (SSSI) owing to its botanical and aquatic plant biodiversity, its recognition as a priority habitat for resident and over-wintering birdlife, and its 'lowland wet grassland' – and let's not forget its salmon and sea trout.

Perversely, perhaps, some of the most botanically species-rich land lies within walled tracks and roadsides, safe from livestock pressures.

Extensive coniferous plantations – Black's, Gill Pasture and Wild Share – may appear 'boring' and species-poor but the first two, at least, support badger, roe deer, fox and breeding buzzard.

1

Origins

Exploration by Victorian antiquarians and modern cave archaeologists has shown that the Settle area has been occupied for millennia, like most of the Dales. Horseshoe Cave at the southern end of Attermire Scar yielded fragments of human bone which may date to the Early Neolithic period (c. 4000-3500 BC) while in nearby Attermire Cave finds dated to the early Roman period include a bronze brooch and a red jasper intaglio (an inscribed gemstone); the thinking is that what was found here and in other local caves is suggestive of cult activity by civilian groups who migrated here with the Roman military machine but stayed on. [2] There is no doubt that the native population who farmed Settle under the Romans carried on their lives afterwards in much the same way, even when new migrants filtered in from the east up the Aire valley and through the Aire-Wenning gap and began establishing themselves amongst the local population in the early seventh century. These were the Angles (we did not have any Saxons here) who spoke a language or a series of dialects that slowly developed into Old English (OE).

The dominance of OE place-names in the Settle area (see the Place-names section) shows that Angles settled here in significant numbers but this does not mean they drove the native Britons out: the story is far more complex than used to be thought. During the later ninth century other bands of migrants arrived and intermingled – Viking Danes from the east, Viking Norse from the west. Settle in what is called the 'early medieval' period (410-1066) was a multi-cultural society with a host of dialects, languages and cultures. [3] Only one major British place-name has survived in the Settle area, namely Cammock, the glacial drumlin alongside the Ribble south of Penny Bridge. The study of place-names is a veritable minefield that needs negotiating with extreme care: most names were not recorded before Domesday Book in 1086, and referred back to 1066, so we must be careful not to jump to the conclusion that names then were the same as in the seventh, eighth or ninth centuries.

What do we know of Settle in 1066 or 1086? Craven – or *Cravescire* in Old English – existed under the Angles but even in 1086 it was not fully part of Yorkshire but lay within the frontier zone between England and Scotland. There were two separate manors in what is now Settle parish. In the southern manor, called *Anele*, Bu was the chief tenant of Edwin, the Anglo-Saxon earl of Mercia. Bu was assessed as having three carucates of land for tax purposes, a carucate being the equivalent of the area that could be ploughed by a team of eight oxen in one season, meaning that Anley, as it is now, *may* have had three plough teams which would suggest a large population. Bu's settlement was probably on what is now Old Anley, above Anley Crag between Lodge Road and Cleatop. His manor would have included Cleatop and Mearbeck. The manorial system required all tenants to take their grain to the lord's corn mill – the soke mill – and Bu's would have been sited at Runley Bridge, between the present B6480 and the Ribble.

The rest of what is now Settle, *Setel* in 1066, was held by Bu of Earl Tostig, King Harold's brother, also assessed at three carucates plus another two held directly by the crown. The site of the soke mill is not known for certain but it may have been on the Giggleswick side of the Ribble. In 1086 both manors were held by Roger of Poitou as overlord, an enormously powerful Norman grandee and landowner for whom this then-remote area would surely have been amongst his lowest priorities. The equally powerful de Percy family were granted the manors of Settle and Giggleswick after Roger carelessly lost all his English estates after rebelling against the king in 1102.

Richard de Percy added to his holdings here by purchasing *Clethop* (Cleatop) with Cleatop Wood, probably within Anley manor, followed by *Allestedes* (Halsteads) and *Cambok* (Cammock), probably part of Settle manor, with his eastern boundary being along Long Preston Moor Road (Map 2). He retained the soke mill at Runley.

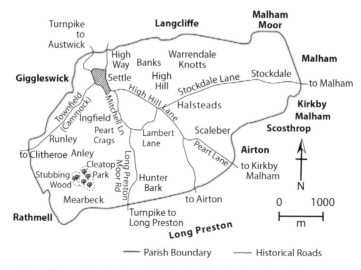

Map 2: The modern Settle parish showing historical roads and place-names

A royal decree from before 1168 granted to tenants of Settle (including Anley) common rights of pasturage on Scaleber, Settle Banks and Stockdale, though they lost access to Stockdale when it was granted to Sawley Abbey sometime before 1200.

On 12 April 1249 Henry de Percy was granted by Henry III the right to hold a fair and market in Settle every Tuesday 'for ever' in addition to a three-day fair on the 'vigil, day and morrow of St Laurence' (9-11 August), a benefit that in essence still exists today. [4] One immediate effect of this was to reduce the rights and status of Elias of Giggleswick who, amongst other benefits, lost his control of the soke mill on the west bank of the Ribble: the 1249 edict can be taken as the point when Settle began to gain in importance and wealth at the expense of Giggleswick.

As time went on Settle developed into a market centre for the whole area between Ribblehead to the north and Nappa to the south, from Clapham in the west to at least Long Preston in the east. Nothing much of significance is heard of the town until 1319. However, the Yorkshire Quo Warrant Rolls for the year 1293-94 noted that in Settle *sunt furca levate* (gallows [or pillory] have been raised) for the previous eight years, though no one seemed to know who had raised it – or, perhaps, no one admitted it. [5]

On 25 November 1319 the royal court's Close Rolls (records of all grants issued in the name of the Crown) noted that the tenants of Settle and surrounding manors were unable to pay the requisite tax because of depredations caused by Scots raids. Their (wood and thatch) houses had been burned to the ground, their goods destroyed and their livestock and food stocks carried off: they were effectively destitute, though there may have been an element of exaggeration here, designed to invoke a feeling of sympathy among the royal tax authorities.

Sixty years later the Poll Tax returns of 1379 assessed the whole of Settle as liable for 17s. 10d. in tax with fifty of the fifty-two heads of household assessed at the standard rate of one groat (4d.); the other two, probably tradesmen, paid 2s. 6d. In contrast, Giggleswick was assessed at £1 1s. 8d., Stainforth at £1 12s. and Langcliffe at 8s. 4d.: Settle was still a minor settlement. It did not change much for many years. In 1513, though, when every manor was required by royal edict to send a band of men to fight the Scots at Flodden Field, thirty-four men of Settle were listed on the Muster Roll. Giggleswick sent twenty, Stainforth seventeen and Langcliffe nine.

In 1537 Settle witnessed a major change in that the last Percy earl of Northumberland died childless and in disgrace and his possessions around

Settle passed to his nephew, Henry Clifford. To the 'downtrodden' tenantry it would have made no difference who was lording over them. Prior to this, when Clifford was steward to Percy, the 1522 Loan Book listed fifty men of Settle eligible to pay tax (Giggleswick thirty-seven). [6] This compares with forty-nine in the Lay Subsidy of 1543 and fifty-one in that of 1545.

Law and order was maintained in Settle by the manor court which sat at specified intervals and laid down laws – or paines – and heard complaints brought against individual tenants who had infringed what the court deemed appropriate. The court sat at Cleatop in the time when a Percy was lord of the manor. [7] A common – and perhaps understandable – infringement was cutting greenwood (ie wood from living trees) in the lord's wood. At a sitting of 1557, for instance, forty men were amerced for this, including Settle's William and John Wildman. Each was fined 2d. [8] The effectiveness of manor court rulings, or perhaps the contempt felt towards the court, is illustrated by the appearance before the court the next year of both men for the same offence. They must have been a lively pair as John was hauled up at that same sitting for illegally ploughing someone else's land and William for failing to settle a bill for various goods he had purchased. To put the system into context, amercements (fines) were seen as an important source of income for the lord rather than just legal penalties for offences committed.

In 1600 Walter Wilson was brought before the court as he had (legally) set out his stall in Settle market to display his iron wares but had (illegally) erected a wood and cloth canopy over it so high that it blocked views of other stalls.

Before this, however, another change had taken place that did have a huge impact on Settle's more prominent tenants: in 1579 the Cliffords felt obliged to lease out many of their tenements to the sitting tenants because the earl's profligate ways had reduced the family to straightened circumstances. In essence, this was the beginning of the end for the manorial system hereabouts. Furthermore, in 1616 the 4th earl (or his steward) decided they had no option other than to sell their estate between Cleatop and Ingfield though they retained the manor. In 1643, however, the last of the Clifford earls of Cumberland died without male issue so his interests passed via Lady Anne Clifford to her daughter Margaret. She married the 2nd Earl of Cork, soon to be 1st Earl of Burlington. The Boyle male line also became extinct on the 3rd earl's death in 1753; his youngest daughter had married William Cavendish, heir to the 4th Duke of Devonshire, in 1748 so the lordship of the manor of Settle (and others) passed to him. He inherited the dukedom in 1755 and the manor has remained in the family ever since.

By this time Settle was beginning to show signs of real economic progress, as evidenced by comparing tax assessments for 1602; [9] Settle as a whole was assessed at 10s. compared to 16s. 8d. for Leeds, 8s. 4d. for Bradford and a paltry 3s. 9d. for Sheffield. In c. 1620 the soke mill at Runley was rebuilt which suggests that the output of grain was, to say the least, buoyant.

From Settle's Anglian origins – assuming that it was not a pre-existing settlement renamed by Anglian incomers – the extent of ploughland, if aggregated, points to a not insignificant population, of maybe fifty households, even then. On level ground early ploughland is visible even today as broad undulations – ridge and furrow. Crops were planted on the drier ridges and the furrows acted as drains by lowering the water table below the ridge tops. On sloping land systems of terraces – lynchets – evolved or were created by the action of the plough.

A flight of lynchets above Dog Meadow

Stones were grubbed out of new ploughlands and used to make walls. This stone had fallen from a collapsed section of wall above Dog Meadow. It shows scratch marks made by a plough as it passed over the stone lying flat just below the surface (200mm scale)

Ridge and furrow can be seen today between Watery Lane and the railway; vague hints of broad ridge and furrow can even be discerned in certain light conditions on the rugby club's first-team pitch. Excellent flights of lynchets can be seen on Cammock, above Dog Meadow allotments and above the former Upper Settle reservoir. At the upper (north) end of this last set of lynchets are the remnants of a most remarkable wall, built of massive recumbent (lying) boulders.

A possible medieval wall at New Field

Above this wall, extending north to High Hill Lane and east to Lambert Lane is a large area, originally one enclosure bounded by substantial walls but later sub-divided by obviously more recent walls. This was New Field, 'new' in the sense that it came after what was there before but in no way new to us. It was in existence at least in the sixteenth century, and was probably medieval, and represented an extension of Settle's ploughlands to cope with an increase in population. In parts, along the southern edge and alongside High Hill Lane, it still stands to its original height of c. 2m. On the death of William Cookeson in 1603 his possessions were disposed of under the aegis of the manor court and they included a 'close called New Field' which he had held on a term of 5000 years, a very common period of lease in times past.

By the start of the seventeenth century we can envisage Settle as a place beginning to burst forth, slowly transforming from a mere village of farmers with the odd tradesman to a centre of trade and commerce, a place where its inhabitants had the optimism and drive to take it to new heights. The next chapter considers how this growth evolved.

2

Growth

Progress in the first half of the seventeenth century was stumbling, and brought to an effective halt by the Civil War and the Cromwellian interlude, but the restoration of the monarchy in 1660 acted as a catalyst – not just in Settle, of course – for renewed optimism and the release of previously entrapped energies. Would-be entrepreneurs, many tenant farmers and those with a vision for the future felt secure for the first time in almost a generation and keen to invest in whatever their enterprise was. This economic regeneration was mirrored in scientific and social change; in short it provided fertile ground for growth. Change was not immediate but gradual and perceptible. The effectively-defunct manor court's roles were gradually hived off to the bylawgreaves, four members of the community who were elected annually to maintain order, though this system had itself become defunct by 1800 at the latest to be replaced by the pre-existing system of constables appointed from local households for a term of one year.

A 1679 tax assessment, levied to pay for military expenditure, affected eight Settle residents and their level of liability contrasts markedly with the Tudor ones discussed earlier. Among them were John Lawson of Lodge (17s.) and John Preston of Mearbeck, both farmers of substance; John Cookeson of the *Naked Man Inn* and Barrel Sykes farm (17s. 3d.); and Roger and James Armitstead (16s. and 14s. respectively).

The latter decades of the seventeenth century saw major change in Settle's housing stock. Swept away were many of the old thatched cottages and farmhouses to be replaced with solid stone-built structures which, in a way, were expressions of the sense of optimism by then current in rural society. Settle spread physically as well, and some of what had been outlying farms were swallowed up within the town. Inns were developed (see Chapter 8) and new trades established. Evidence of growth can be teased out: look closely at some of the houses and the late seventeenth-century date-stones above the doors. Some of the buildings were further modified or even rebuilt in the late eighteenth or nineteenth century but retained the earlier date-stone. Farms of some substance included Cob Castle in Upper Settle (the Armitsteads, 1663); Cragdale on Victoria Street; what is now more than one dwelling, namely the range at the foot of Albert Hill; the Kidd family's farm higher up Albert Hill; and what is now partly Primrose House, with a blocked up coach-house arch, also on Victoria Street.

A former farmhouse at the foot of Albert Hill, with altered mullioned windows

Evidence of Settle's rebuilding programme is also to be seen in many buildings re-worked later on: a walk around Settle's central Conservation Area looking closely at buildings reveals vertical straight joints in the masonry where the original building was extended, blocked-up doorways or mullioned windows. Look, for example at Jessamine Cottage next to the Co-op with its blocked first-floor doorway, or at both front and rear elevations of the flower shop at the top of Cheapside.

The rear elevation of the flower shop on Cheapside, showing seventeenth-century mullioned windows, a fine door head, a ground-floor blocked window and a top-to-bottom ragged joint showing where the building was altered

In 1708 a petition was successfully made on behalf of the then lord of the manor, the Earl of Burlington, to the court of Queen Anne for 'several other new Faires to be held yearly'. Trade in the Settle area had grown to the extent that informal markets were being held in the town without consent and without paying tolls thereby denying the lord an important source of manorial income. Granting of the new market rights regulated matters while catering for Settle's growing commercial base: some fairs were for livestock, others for 'goods, wares and merchandizes', and yet others for a whole array of products animate and inanimate. [10] At this time out of Settle's total area of 4490 acres (1820 hectares) only 8 per cent was under the plough and less than 2 per cent under cereal crops like oats and barley The balance was made up of legumes (peas and beans), and flax or hemp: the historical field name for the area between Upper Settle and Greenfoot car park was Hemplands.

An old and rickety house behind the Shambles in 1864, showing the wooden portico for its first-floor entry (Horner Collection)

Several worthies included Settle on their Grand Tours of England. Richard Pococke (1704-65), ostensibly a bishop, anthropologist and inveterate traveller, who visited the town on 26 July 1760, described Settle as a 'pretty great thoroughfare, and has a small manufacture of knit stockings'. [11] The poet, Thomas Gray (1716-71) approached Settle from the west, like Pococke, in October 1769, staying two nights, and his impression was that Settle was a 'small market town standing directly under a rocky fell ... with mostly old and low' buildings which had 'little wooden porticos' at the front. [12] None of these porticos has survived though we know the former first-floor doorways to the flower shop on Cheapside and to Jessamine Cottage did have them, as did a dwelling on the upper side of Market Place, long since demolished.

Just a few years later the noted Welsh naturalist, antiquarian and traveller Thomas Pennant (1726-98) also visited Settle. [13] Sadly, he was not totally impressed by what he saw in 1773. On the positive side, he had 'dined at the neatest and most comfortable little inn I ever was at, rendered more agreeable by the civility and attention of the landlady': he did not name the inn. On the neutral side, he reported that Settle was a 'market town, and has a small trade in knit-worsted stockings, which are made here from two to five shillings a pair' and 'Numbers of coiners and filers lived about the place, at this time entirely out of work' as a result of new legislation. On the arguably negative side, however, he considered Settle to be 'exactly resembling a shabby French town with a "place" in the middle'.

Edward Dayes (1763-1804), watercolourist, teacher of that other notable painter Thomas Girtin, and influencer of J.M.W. Turner, undertook a journey through Derbyshire and Yorkshire visiting Settle in 1803. [14] He saw the town in a very different light from Pennant. Though he thought it 'seated in the midst of barren hills ... Romantic as the situation may be, the town itself is equally so', romantic, that is, and the houses were in his opinion 'whimsical, picturesque, odd'. He did not mean that in a disparaging way. Like Gray, Dayes also noted the number of buildings around the Market Place with external access to the first floor.

In the 1760s a young man, who was born in the West Indies to plantation owners and sent back to England at the age of six to be brought up in Furness, came to Settle. [15] This was John Coakley Lettsom (1744-1815; see Chapter 9) and in 1761 he came here to take up an apprenticeship with Abraham Sutcliffe, apothecary, later becoming a renowned London surgeon (see Chapter 9). Lettsom stayed here for five years and was minded to record what he saw of Settle as a hand-drawn map that he dedicated 'To Joseph Rathbone of Liverpool, this Sketch of **Settle** in Yorkshire: is offered By his Friend **J C Lettsom**' (Map 3).

Sutcliffe's house, at the corner of Cheapside and Duck (now Duke) Street, is depicted prominently on the map with Elbow Lane bounding it on two sides. The south section of this lane was long since infilled with a building but the east section survives as the narrow and dark ginnel that is affectionately known, for perhaps obvious reasons, as 'Spooky Alley'. Lettsom also marked the row of buildings owned by the Birkbeck family (see Chapter 9) on Cheapside. Oddly, perhaps, he did not mark any inns. Many of the streets have changed their names since his day: we will return to this in subsequent chapters.

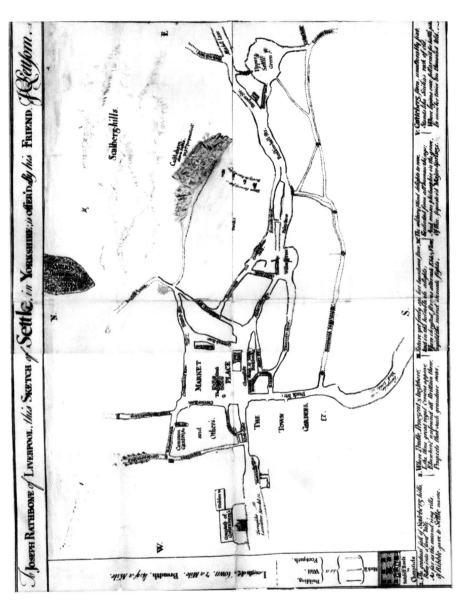

Map 3: John Lettsom's map of Settle, 1761-65
(reproduced with permission and © Ironbridge Gorge Museum Trust)

Anne Lister, of Shibden Hall, Halifax, passed through Settle in July 1824, setting off

> from Settle (the Golden Lion now styled Hartley's Hotel) at 9.25 ...
> Settle is a romantic or rather foreign-like looking town. The Market
> Place has something of the air of a grande place abroad. This morning
> was the fortnight fair and the market was full of sheep penned in
> divisions; and there were a great many head of cattle. [16]

No settlement can grow without strong communication links with the outside world: the next chapter addresses Settle's external connections.

3

Connections

Legislation concerning roads effectively dates from the reign of Henry I (1100-35) whose court issued an edict ordering all major roads (*via magna* or *via regia*) to be maintained wide enough for two wagons to pass. [17] In 1285 the Statute of Winchester further ordered all woodland to be cut back 200 feet (61m) on either side to avoid places where 'a man may lurk to do hurt'. The first map to show major roads is known as Gough's Map but only because the eighteenth-century antiquarian and topographer, Richard Gough, bequeathed it to the Bodleian Library. No one knows when it was drawn, but its emphasis on routes into Wales suggests it may be from the reign of Edward I, thus c. 1280 though the surviving map is most probably a copy made between 1355 and 1366. [18] Roads were marked as straight red lines and were shown connecting significant settlements on most major routes: one headed north via Grantham, Doncaster, Bradford and Skipton before heading through Settle, Bentham and Kirkby Lonsdale to Kendal. The distance from Skipton to Settle is marked as ten. The unit of measurement was French miles *(lieues)* whose length varied considerably (as did pre-statute English miles first introduced c. 1675). On the A65 it is 16 miles (c. 26km) so the medieval *via magna* appears shorter than the modern road. In fact the medieval route took a different line in several places. Approaching Settle it followed what are now Long Preston Moor Road and Mitchell Lane over Hunter Bark (see Map 2).

The medieval route descending from Hunter Bark towards Settle

The medieval road was for many years referred to as the 'Judges Road' because the King's Justices rode it on their regular circuits. The road dropped down the steep hill into Upper Settle, where sunken holloways suggest more than one actual line, headed through town and down Kirkgate to what is now Sowarth Field industrial estate. Here it diverged. The original line crossed the Ribble at Kendalman's Ford, though travellers must have been held up many a time by high water levels. This name hints at the major packhorse trade from Kendal through Settle to Skipton and beyond. The route can still be traced on foot (with difficulty) as a narrow, fenced path adjacent to the Creamery terminating at the river bank; on the opposite side of the river a narrow, walled, former trackway continues the line of the road for a short distance.

Kendalman's Ford, looking east

The alternative route paralleled the east bank of the Ribble to Settle Bridge. In 1531 the Statute of Bridges repeated an earlier edict that towns and shires were required to maintain bridges on major routes. Settle Bridge was first recorded in a Percy rental from 1498, so the manorial authorities here were ahead of the game. What is not recorded is whether the stone bridge was a replacement for an earlier wooden structure. In 1662 it was repaired at the charge of the whole West Riding, and was included in the magisterial *Account of all the Bridges in the West Riding in the County of York surveyed* in 1752. [19] Further repairs were effected in 1674, 1683 and 1697. In 1783 it was more than doubled in width.

The heavily-ribbed arches supporting the medieval part of Settle Bridge

There was no direct road from Market Place to Settle Bridge until 1804 but a footpath had existed through Northfield since who knows when, serving as the Church Footway for Settle folk to attend the parish church of St Alkelda in Giggleswick. The manor court clearly became vexed by the misuse of this footpath and in 1680 a fine was levied against 'anyone who rides of the Northfield' – it was footway not a bridle road. John Ogilby, His Majesty's Cosmographer and Geographic Printer, produced a series of road maps in strip form published in 1675 as *Britannia*. [20] Drawn at a scale of 1 inch to the mile, and with annotations and line drawings, his maps are a delight. For the journey from Long Preston to Settle he wrote:

> ... you enter a Moor, and ascend an Hill of 10 Furlongs height, and presently descend 8 Furlongs at the bottom of which you enter Settle, a town of good Accommodation ... At the end whereof over a Stone Bridg ... [21]

Incidentally, today's Kirkgate does not follow the line of the medieval Kirkgate for most of its length. When groundworks were underway for building the supermarket on Kirkgate/Bond Lane in 2000-01 the trackbed of the original road was exposed (but, sadly, not recorded) where the car park now is. From the former *Spread Eagle Inn* (see Chapter 8) it made a beeline for Kendalman's Ford, turning sharp right at the bottom to head towards Settle Bridge on what used to be called Old Road. [22]

Apart from the main east-west road, several other through roads converged on Settle. High Hill Lane connected the town with Malhamdale and Pennant, who we met earlier, described how he 'descended an exceedingly tedious and steep road' into Settle which is most likely this route. There was a road from Settle to Clitheroe which followed the present road towards Settle roundabout but curved away to the south before Runley Bridge to follow the east bank of the Ribble fording it below Long Stream Barn. [23] A third road headed northwards from Settle: this was Highway not the present B6479, Lan[g]cliff Lane in Lettsom's time. In the late nineteenth century Highway continued eastwards along what is now called Castleberg Lane. [24]

In 1697, by Act of Parliament, Surveyors of the Highways across the country were required to erect guide posts on the King's Highways to point the direction to the nearest market towns, and many of these had a pointing hand. The West Riding responded to the Act in 1700 by ordering 'stoops to be sett up in Cross highways with a stone or post' and the names of the next town in each direction. If pointing hands were not etched into the posts, the traveller knew to turn right, while looking at the side of the post with the name of his/her destination town. One such guide post can be seen at the top of Runley Bridge lane: one face reads 'To Settle 1 M', another 'To Clitheroe 17 M', the third 'To Skipton 13 M', while the fourth side is hidden from view. However, etched into it are the word SETTLE and two (originally three) circular flowers. It is not set in its original position as this lane was not a historical routeway; it may have stood to the west of Runley Bridge where the Clitheroe road curved away. The Skipton face has a hand pointing to the left and the Clitheroe face one pointing to the right so it is aligned correctly in its current position and would also make sense if set in its original position further west.

Guide post at Runley Bridge

24

Another old milestone is set into the wall on School Hill below Zion Chapel. There is some doubt as to whether Victoria Street was the historical main road down from Hunter Bark or what are now Castleberg Lane and School Hill. If the latter, the stone could be more or less *in situ* but, if not, it has clearly been removed. It reads from top to bottom: To London 236 miles, Kirkby Lonsdale 17, Hawes 22, Skipton 16, Lancaster 26. To have headed for London or Skipton meant going uphill, and for Kirkby Lonsdale or Lancaster downhill through Market Place. The inclusion of Hawes might suggest the traveller was being directed along what is now Castleberg Lane but, historically the road ahead and behind, on the level, was called Highway which would have taken our traveller through Langcliffe and onwards via Ribblehead.

Milestone on School Hill

A national campaign to improve major roads grew in strength through the early eighteenth century with the creation of turnpike trusts charged with either repairing or re-routing existing roads. The historical east-west road through Settle was described as 'very ruinous and in Great Decay, and is not only impassable for Wheel Carriages, but is very dangerous for Travellers'. [25] Thus was enacted the Keighley to Kendal Turnpike Trust: the initial trustees meetings were held at the home of Robert Johnson, innkeeper of the *Talbot Inn*, and attendees included the Birkbecks, Farrer of the Ingleborough Estate in Clapham and Ingleby from Lawkland Hall. The turnpike road abandoned the hazardous route over Hunter Bark, from 1753, and followed the line that is now the A65 from Long Preston to Settle entering town along Duke Street.

John Birtwhistle, noted cattle dealer, was contracted to construct the road from Settle to Long Preston at 11s. 9d. per rood (16½ feet) laying stone 15 inches

(400mm) thick and building an arched bridge over 'Rundley Beck'. He had still not completed the job in 1758, five years later. The Minutes of the Trustees meeting recorded on 20 May 1760 'Many items of trouble' with him and on 31 March 1761 'Suit to be begun against John Birtwhistle'. He sounds to have been an awkward character.

It became compulsory in 1767 to erect mileposts on all turnpike roads though the cast-iron ones that still grace many of our roads date from the 1890s: in 1892 the West Riding County Council placed orders for hundreds of them to replace existing turnpike mileposts. On the Keighley to Kendal road William Towler of Globe Foundry, Horsforth in Leeds, won the contract to supply the cast-iron faces at a unit cost of £1 18s. [26] The original turnpike mileposts were of stone and in 1760 a man by the name of Knowles was charged with providing 'horse-in-stones between Settle and Kirkby as shall be necessary'. [27]

A cast-iron Towler milepost at Anley: 'Keighley and Kendal Road Settle
Skipton 14¾ miles Keighley 24 miles Settle ¾ mile Kendal 30 miles'

The original turnpike headed down Kirkgate to Settle Bridge but it was re-routed in 1804 to avoid the two awkward right-angled corners. The new line followed what is now Church Street, and was constructed '13 yards between the fences, 10 yards to be stoned, the crown to be 14 inches thick ... the whole to be covered with 2 inches of good gravel', all at a cost of £2 7s. 6d. per rood. [28] A milestone, with exactly the same destinations and distances as the School Hill stone is set into a garden wall near the cenotaph. It cannot have been here before 1804.

Milestone on Church Street

The original intention had been to erect a toll bar on the east side of Settle Bridge but it was quickly decided that too many travellers would bypass it by using Highway or Kendalman's Ford. Instead, in 1823, a toll bar was sited at Runley Bridge and this proved to be the most lucrative of all five bars between Ingleton and Coniston Cold. In 1861 the toll keeper was Ann Gill, aged 25.

Runley Bridge Toll Bar Cottage

Had two other connections come to fruition, Settle would be a very different place now: think Skipton, or even Keighley. In 1780 proposals were put forward to construct a canal – the Parkfoot Canal – from Stackhouse via Austwick and Ingleton to join the Wenning at Park Foot, Burton in Lonsdale. [29] Opposition from affected landowners prevented it from going ahead. Prior to that, in 1769, there were ambitious plans to build the 24km-long Settle Canal leaving the still-to-be-built Leeds and Liverpool Canal from near Barnoldswick. Prime movers in this scheme were Abraham Sutcliffe and William Birkbeck who tried to sell the benefits of being able to bring in fire-coal (for domestic use) and lime-coal (for lime kilns) and to send out quicklime, slate and flags from Helwith Bridge, timber and wool. What the promoters did not bargain for was vociferous opposition from Thomas Lister of Gisburn Hall who adopted the 'over my dead body' approach. The plans got short shrift in parliament on 28 February 1774. One pamphlet from the opposition was rather scathing about Settle. [30] It described the town as 'but a very small place – has only one shop – no kind of manufactures or trade of consequence either at or near it – is surrounded on almost every side with mountains and barren rocks'. Reading between the lines, there is more than a hint here of social disharmony among Settle's luminaries. Sutcliffe and Birkbeck were Quakers, barred from the professions but very successful businessmen and entrepreneurs; Lister and other opponents represented the landed gentry from 'proper' places of worship. A letter, dated 8 March 1774, addressed to an unknown recipient, made their position clear: there was no possibility that their landed interests would ever be eroded by commercial interests.

Had the Settle Canal come into being, the idea was for it to terminate in a basin where Greenfoot car park is now. The tall block on the left of the roadway from the car park into town is called Liverpool House. This writer remembers from the 1980s a large framed map – an original map – on the wall of the ground floor when it was used as a tea shop. It was map of the proposed canal route and, it was said, Liverpool House was built to serve as the Settle offices.

Liverpool House

Commercial interests eventually came to overrule the landed: in 1849/50 the 'Little North Western' Railway was opened connecting Leeds with Lancaster and Morecambe and the first Settle Station (now Giggleswick Station) was built. There was no road link from town to station so in 1849 the company built a road – New Road – from Duke Street, demolishing New Inn Yard and its outbuildings in the process, crossing the Ribble at Penny Bridge (the initial toll charge was 1d.). [31] Twenty years later, in November 1869, the first sod was cut for the Settle-Carlisle Railway at Anley Crag – on Birkbeck land – and the present Settle Station opened in 1876. Its extensive area of sidings boosted Settle's economy enormously; however, in 1970 goods facilities were removed.

A final connection – a disconnection maybe – came in December 1988 when Settle bypass was opened. With the exponential growth in traffic since then one wonders how the town centre could have coped with constant gridlock at the *Royal Oak* pinch point: it was bad enough in the 1980s.

4

Commerce

By the latter half of the eighteenth century Settle's physical and economic growth had increased markedly, and it is clear there was a palpable optimism in the air. Scaleber, High Scar and Settle Banks had historically been stinted pastures grazed in common by those tenant farmers who had rights to put a specified number of sheep and cattle to pasture. In 1759 all three commons were enclosed and carved up into individual enclosures; it was a kind of privatisation whereby the tenants could now invest in their parts and improve land quality. In 1804 High Hill and Halstead Pasture were similarly carved up. [32] In 1768 Attermire had also been enclosed, tenanted by Thomas Carr, and an indenture included the creation of a new road from High Hill Bottom with a 'Breadth of Twelve feet and no more'. [33] Farmers were no longer constrained by a lack of investment or will to improve land that was grazed in common (why should I commit any money if you won't?) and this was the catalyst for a step forward in land and stock management which, in turn, provided the funds from increased profits to improve farm buildings and livestock.

Within the town itself trade and commerce boomed and broadened out. By the end of the eighteenth century Settle had dressmakers, tanners, boot, shoe and clog makers, black- and whitesmiths, masons, saddlers, corn millers, rope makers, millwrights, tallow chandlers and cotton manufacturers. In 1822 the town had at least thirty-three retail shops, twenty-three merchants and tradesmen; eight wagon carriers operated regular, timetabled routes through the Dales and to Kendal, Lancaster, Leeds, Halifax, Guisborough, north-east Lancashire and even London, illustrating how much trade the town had to offer. Then there were those in the professions – banks, legal services, medicine and schools, plus innholders and licensed victuallers. In 1834 there were six blacksmith businesses, nine boot and shoe or clog makers, six butchers, forty-nine shopkeepers, seven tailors, five stone masons, three surgeons, five painters and glaziers, five insurance agents and a rope maker on Rope Walk (just beyond the old Catholic church). [34] We can neatly sum up the new spirit of endeavour by referring to one property on Victoria Street. Underberg, formerly Primrose House, has a date-stone from a much earlier house than stands there today, namely '1664 IEW' – John and Elizabeth Wildman. They were successful farmers as well as traders and merchants and after her husband died in 1669 Elizabeth married into the prominent and wealthy Paley family which demonstrates the Wildmans' enhanced status.

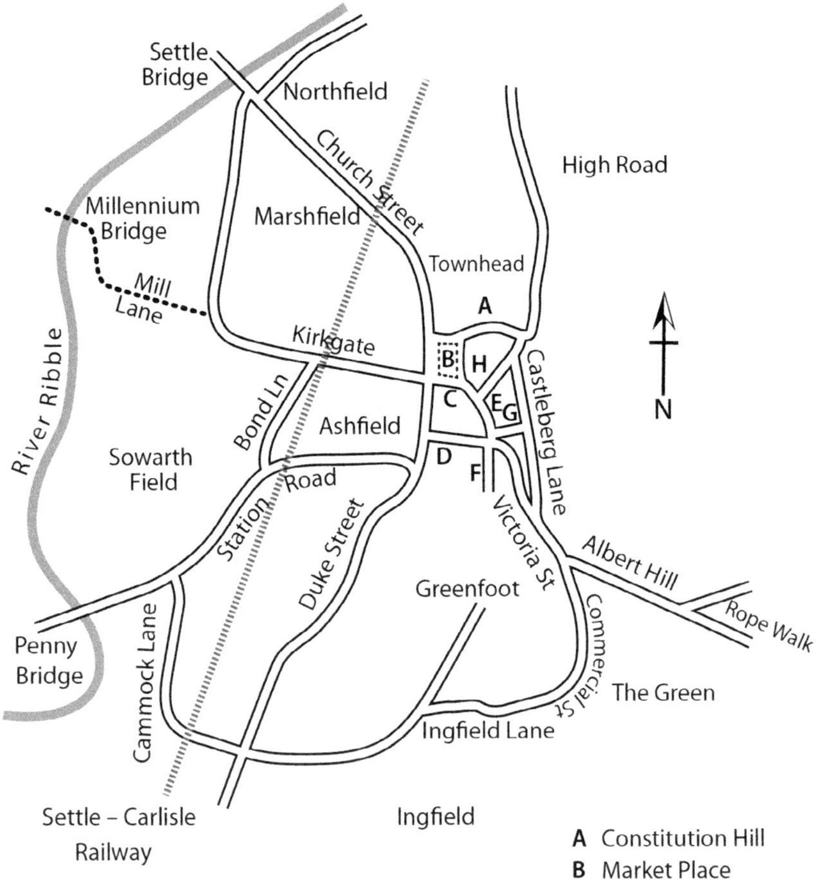

Map 4: Settle's street pattern

A Constitution Hill
B Market Place
C Cheapside
D Chapel Street
E High Street
F Chapel Square
G Well Hill
H Castle Hill

We can link farming and commerce in other ways, for example Settle's multiple tradesmen who relied on livestock for their raw materials: livestock dealers, slaughterhouse workers, tanners, curriers, butchers, boot and shoe makers, saddlers, tallow chandlers. The last slaughterhouse, towards the east end of Bond Lane, was operational until the 1970s and only demolished for housing development in the early 1990s.

The Castleberg Lane slaughterhouse 'ten minutes before the building came crashing down' on 27 July 1971 (courtesy Barbara Middleton)

Another slaughterhouse, next to the primary school playground on Castleberg Lane and now the parking area for Old School Close, was still operational up to the Second World War much to the upset of the children.

Inset: Bark crushing gear in Upper Settle tannery (Riley Collection)

Tan pits in Upper Settle tannery (Riley Collection)

Certainly up to the end of the eighteenth century Settle was the centre of a major tanning business with tanneries at Catterall (Giggleswick), Mearbeck, Langcliffe, Sherwood House (Stainforth) and Settle itself. In 1594 William Newby, a Settle tanner, accused a customer of failing to pay for a quantity of leather, confirming that it was a long-established industry here. It is said that the Talbot Inn was the preferred meeting place for dealers and tanners to do business.

NOTICE.

SHEEP & CATTLE FAIR AT SETTLE.

THERE WILL BE A FAIR

AT SETTLE, FOR

SHEEP,

ON THURSDAY OCTOBER 8th 1857,

AND THE DAY AFTER

FRIDAY THE 9th OCTOBER, FOR

CATTLE.

These Fairs will be held annually and will always be on The THURSDAY and FRIDAY before the OCTOBER FALKIRK TRYST.

An advertisement for Settle stock fair, 1857
(Settle Chronicle and North Ribblesdale Advertiser)

In 1800, however, it was claimed that the leather trade here was in decline though fortnightly fairs were still held for cattle and leather goods; yet the tannery at the foot of The Green in Upper Settle, possibly opened c. 1792, only closed in the twentieth century.

In 1844, according to the tithe apportionment, the Upper Settle tanyard was occupied by Matthew Whittam but owned by the Rev'd Henry Dawson and his brother. Another tanyard, between School Hill, Castleberg Lane and Victoria Street, was owned by Alice Thornber and worked by her and John Bland. The process of tanning hides was, to say the least, messy and the smells, especially in summer, must have been intolerable for local residents: human urine, dog dung and pigeon droppings mixed with lime were all part of the mix. The process of preparing tanned hides into leather was undertaken by curriers – Currier Cottage on Victoria Street keeps alive the memory of this once significant trade.

The smithy by Bowskills Yard, 1932, with local 11-year old Ernest Cokell lending a hand (Horner Collection)

Blacksmiths were in constant demand in an economy where horses dominated passenger traffic, wagon carriage and farming and the numbers in Settle fluctuated from two in 1822 to seven in 1851. The Bowskill family were prominent cattle dealers, merchants and blacksmiths, and Bowskills Yard off Castleberg Lane perpetuates their name. In 1767 John Bowskill occupied a 'cottage and smithy' at the south end of Duke Street and in 1834 and 1851 William was described as a master blacksmith. [35] A second smithy was run by Bartholomew Armitstead who, in 1777, occupied a 'new Dwelling House or Shop commonly called a Smiths Shop' in Settle adjacent to a 'Shoeing Place'; and only a year later another legal transaction referred to a blacksmith's shop 'now converted' into a dwelling. Clearly, he had translocated from the old smithy to the new in 1777. [36]

Exactly when the smithy at Bowskills Yard/Castleberg Lane was set up is unknown but the chances are, given its location, that it was the Bowskills'; it was certainly there in 1767 when John Bowskill was in charge. It still has the forge equipment intact but is no longer regularly used as a smithy and has not seen a horse for many a year.

Settle market, c. 1900 (Horner Collection)

As we saw earlier, Settle has held regular markets since 1249. By the end of the eighteenth century the system had been rationalised to the present Tuesday market, fortnightly livestock fairs serving butchers mainly from Lancashire, and a larger annual fair. Livestock sales dealt with horses, cattle, sheep and geese. These apart, leather, stockings, yarn, woollen cloth and oatmeal were the main products along with wheat, beans, peas and barley.

A goose fair in full swing, 1900-10 (Horner Collection)

A friend of this writer once recounted how, as a teenager in the late 1930s, he helped his grandfather drive their geese through a bed of wet tar at their farm at Helwith Bridge before driving them (on foot) to market in Lancaster, a task that must have been fraught with frustration but rich in humour.

The medieval market cross was taken down c. 1870 and replaced with the present fountain.

One integral element of Settle's late eighteenth-century economic and demographic growth was a building boom; dwellings and warehouses were squeezed into vacant plots, no matter how small or irregularly shaped. Also evident from this time was the development of 'yards' which became such a feature of Settle, with some still surviving in names like Howson's Yard off Market Place and Twisleton's Yard at the bottom of Albert Hill, bought by James Twisleton in 1832.

*The yard hiding behind
Kirkgate*

Some still survive as open areas but the names on the ground have been 'lost', for instance, Poole's Yard in Upper Settle and King William Yard between High Street and Castle Hill. Old Stables Yard next to Rock House on Castle Hill, entered through an archway, was the workplace in the mid nineteenth century of a tallow chandler, probably Peter Skirrow (aged 52) recorded as living on Kirkgate in 1851, and John Preston (aged 20) who lived with his parents on Duke Street. Back Stables Yard was behind the old *Golden Lion Inn* on Cheapside; Back Kirkgate Yard was (probably) the hidden yard to the south of Kirkgate; Tatham's Yard was off High Street as was Talbot Yard; King William Yard was behind the former pub of that name.

*Birkbeck properties on
Cheapside rebuilt from what is
visible of the seventeenth-
century building on the far left.
Note the three white gutter
hoppers. Tatham's building has
the round-headed taking-in
doors and crane*

The Birkbecks rebuilt whatever stood along much of Cheapside. What is now the newsagents was one of their dwellings and the units either side were warehouses and shops. The cast-iron gutter hopper-heads bear the date 'IB 1777' – the date when John Birkbeck had the row rebuilt, heightened and gentrified.

In 1818 William Birkbeck & Co. assigned what is now the outdoor and sportswear shop on Cheapside to John Tatham. [37] The property was described then as an 'extensive Warehouse with the cellar ...'. The two taking-in doors and the crane point to this function. John Tatham & Son traded as family grocers, Italian warehousemen, druggists and general drapers. [38] It may be that they were among the first merchants in the country to operate a mail order system. In the 1851 census return, John Tatham (aged 20) was head of household living with his eight-year old brother, two shop assistants and two live-in house servants.

The Craven Bank had its second home in this impressive building, originally erected by the Birkbecks as dwellings

Until 2018 Settle had four 'traditional' banks but now only two remain. This is fewer than in the 1800s. The first one to be created in Settle was the Birkbeck family's bank which merged with Henry Alcock's Skipton bank, with John Peart of Grassington and Settle as the third element in what became the Craven Banking Co. established in 1791. [39] Until 1817 their bank notes bore an image of Castleberg but thenceforth of the famous Craven heifer. In 1844 the bank was still housed in what is now the shop on the corner of Duke Street and Cheapside. In 1880 it was incorporated as The Craven Bank Ltd, and was absorbed by the Bank of Liverpool in 1906; then, via Martins Bank in 1918, it was later subsumed within Barclays.

The former Craven Savings Bank

In 1818 the Craven Savings Bank was opened on a site that had formerly been a saddler's workshop and dwellings, following national legislation the year before. It was well supported as a concept as local luminaries William Bolland and Benjamin Birkbeck were trustees, the Duke of Devonshire and Earl of Thanet patrons and Lord Ribblesdale the first president. As time passed local savings banks were amalgamated into more efficient business units, which all became the Trustee Savings Bank (TSB) in 1976. How the savings bank based in a room in the Town Hall until 1865 fitted into this is not known.

Bank Buildings on High Street

The third early bank was formed in 1836 as a branch of the Yorkshire District Banking Co. located in Bank Buildings on High Street. In 1870 it moved to the building now occupied by HSBC changing its name to the Yorkshire Banking Co. Eventually it was swallowed up in the Midland Bank group, hence the HSBC link.

Settle's first Co-op shop in Upper Settle in the 1930s. From left to right: Frank James, Horace Patrick and Billy Breaks (courtesy Barbara Middleton)

Inset: A centennial plaque by Settle's War Memorial

Settle Co-op's first shop as it is now. Through the green double doors is the yard which formerly had stables for the Co-op's cart horse(s)

No discussion of Settle's trade and commerce would be complete without mention of the Co-op. The Co-operative movement is often taken as starting with the creation of the Rochdale Pioneers in 1844 but earlier, short-lived, attempts were made to run a shop on co-operative lines – one of them in 1829 in Langcliffe, no less. [40] By 1851 there were thirteen co-operative societies nationwide, and 1400 by the end of the century. In 1861 the Settle Equitable Industrial Co-operative Society was formed, with forty-five members joining at the outset and eighty by the end of its first year. It partly grew out of local distress when imports of cotton from the southern American states were cut off by war leading to mill closures and mass unemployment in the cotton textile industry.

Initially the first Co-op shop in Settle, opened on Victoria Street in 1861, was only open in the evenings but after one year it opened all day. The Society flourished, buying out John Delaney's shop in Langcliffe, extensively refurbishing the Victoria Street shop in 1894, and opening a second grocery shop on Craven Terrace near Bridge End in 1911. [41]

Settle Co-op's shop on Craven Terrace, opened in 1911,
closed c. 1980 and now Kingdom Hall

The Society bought many of the houses in East View on Skipton Road to rent out, and in 1937 the trustees purchased a '30cwt Morris Commercial Lorry' at a cost of £243; arrangements were made with FH Ellis's garage to have it serviced annually – for only 15s! [42] In its early heydays the Co-op issued tokens to members with values ranging from 2d. to £1.

In 1944 further expansion saw the opening of a baker's and confectioner's shop on Duke Street with the bakery in Commercial Yard; in 1953 a butcher's shop was opened on High Street and in 1956 a separate drapery shop was opened in the shop at the corner of High Street and Castle Hill. [43] Retrenchment came in the 1960s: the butcher's shop was shut in 1962 and transferred to the Duke Street shop (now Wholesome Bee), the original Upper Settle shop was shut in 1967; and the trustees meeting of 9 October 1968 approved the merger of the Settle Society with Keighley and Skipton District Co-operative Society. [44] In its new guise, the large shop in Market Place (now a bike shop), opened in 1955 and continued selling drapery, ladies' and men's wear, furniture, electrical goods and hardware until a new and much larger store was opened in the 1970s in what had been the New Vic (or Nuvic) Cinema since 1939 and later a roller skating rink and bingo hall. This is the present Settle Co-op store with its huge rear warehouse built in 1991. The projection room and Art deco screen are still intact in the roof space.

The stump of a possible cast-iron gas retort on the riverside path south of Settle Bridge. The retorts were used in the gas-making process

The mid nineteenth century saw a drive to provide Settle with much-needed street lighting; in 1851 Thomas Brigg bought the grounds to the rear of the *Spread Eagle Inn* and leased it out to the Vegetable Gas Light Company which used fish oil as the raw material – predictably, perhaps, it soon failed because the gas was too expensive to produce. John Tatham was one of the company's founders. [45] The fish oil system was replaced with coal gas production in 1856, with a gasometer behind Victoria Hall, though production was later transferred to Upper Settle; it became the Settle Gas Company in 1896. It was all demolished in 1960. The latest gas works, and gasometers, were sited on the Ribble just north of Penny Bridge on the east bank.

The West Yorkshire Garage in the 1940s (courtesy FH Ellis)

As Settle moved into the motor age, local facilities were established. In what is now a carpet shop on Duke Street stood a petrol station with a cycle and motorbike dealership; and Car and Kitchen in Market Place is so called because it, too, was a filling station (Central Garage). FH Ellis has been a garage on the present site from the early days of motorised vehicles. Initially called the West Yorkshire Garage and Motor Company, it was built in 1909 by two brothers called Lancaster, but sold in 1915 to one of their apprentices, Fred Ellis.

This chapter has discussed trades undertaken in workshops and warehouses; Chapter 5 moves on to consider Settle's larger-scale factory enterprises, its textile mills.

5

Textiles

Settle had a long involvement in textiles, initially in wool but mostly in cotton. An entry in the (royal) Patent Rolls, for 12 June 1348, recorded that Allan Tollere of Settle sold four stones of wool and Walter Bateman, also of Settle, sold the same quantity to Crown-appointed wool merchants. [46] That was trade, though, not manufacture. In 1851, 242 of Settle's residents were employed in spinning or weaving, mostly in cotton. This writer was taught in school that 'Lancashire was cotton and Yorkshire was wool': not in the Dales, though. This was largely the result of the Leeds and Liverpool Canal which enabled importation of raw cotton through Liverpool to wharves in the Barnoldswick area with onward despatch by trains of packhorses. One account, referring to the early nineteenth century, described how in the Settle area 'the sound of the hand-loom might be heard in every village ... and in almost every street. From the town of Settle ... there must have been a considerable output of hand-made fabrics.' [47]

The transition to a textile mill economy in Settle (and Langcliffe) was not always smooth and in 1825-26, for example, there was a severe decline in the local cotton trade with prices paid to piece-work cotton weavers at rock bottom. [48] By 1835, however, Settle had five cotton mills, employing 330 men, women and children. [49] They were Runley Bridge, Dog Kennel, Bridge End, King's and Brennand's Weaving Shed.

Runley Bridge mill in 1990

In 1784 the former corn mill at Runley Bridge was advertised as being 'well situated for spinning cotton wool or flax'. A legal transaction in 1786 involved James Brennand of Settle, merchant, and Henry Coor of Settle, Gent, concerning

'Rundley Close' including buildings and machinery connected with cotton spinning. Two years later another transaction described Brennand as 'Cotton Manufacturer' and concerned 'Runley Cotton Mill', then occupied by John Thornber of Colne, and James and William Thornber and William Bracewell, all of Barnoldswick. [50] In 1795 John Thornber still occupied the mill but by 1803 it was let to Messrs Proctor (or Procter). [51] In 1825 the mill was destroyed by fire though it was still shown on Ordnance Survey mapping of 1847 as 'Runley Bridge Mill (Cotton)'. The tithe apportionment of 1844 listed Alice Thornber as owner-occupier of the mill. By 1850, however, it was purely in agricultural use, owned by the Birkbecks.

The site of Dog Kennel Mill behind the high wall among the trees. The wall has a blocked-up aperture from one of the mill buildings

On the hillside above the allotments is the site of Dog Kennel Mill, another cotton spinning mill. Very little remains of it now, save one high wall with evidence of a former window and Scaleber Cottage opposite the pinfold. An old leat runs along the contours on Meal Bank below Springfield farm tapping into natural springs and the water is (still) carried through a channel underneath the top end of Albert Hill. It fed the mill waterwheel. The culverted tailrace also still carries water downhill through the allotments to Watery Lane. In 1800 Thomas Preston, John Dale, Thomas Shackleton and William Banks, cotton spinners all of Settle, set their signatures to a deed concerning the 'Cotton Mill in Dog Kennel Close'. [52] James Brennand managed the mill from

1788-93 followed by the Thornbers and later by Proctor: the same names keep cropping up. One source connects Faulkner & Co. with this mill in the early 1830s but Thomas Brennand (James's son perhaps) from 1837. [53] The tithe apportionment listed Thomas as owner and occupier of the mill. By 1854 it had ceased production.

Radcliffe Yard, Albert Hill

An assignment from 1778 concerned a parcel of ground in Upper Settle called 'Sadlers Close' or 'Walk mill Close'. [54] It was not located but does suggest there was a walk-mill there. A walk-mill was a fulling mill within which woollen cloth was soaked in a tank of hot water and fuller's-earth, and possibly human urine, for the workers either to stamp it with their bare feet or to pummel it with their bare hands or a wooden pommel. It was a boring, laborious and unpleasant way to spend a long day. It is known that Charles Ratcliffe ran a textile mill in Upper Settle; immediately above Twisleton's Yard on Albert Hill is a long narrow plot that used to be called Radcliffe Yard and within it is a long narrow building that was called 'Jane Etherington's Radcliffe Yard Lodging House' in the 1891 census, with sixteen lodgers in residence, and 'Lodging House Yard' in 1871, but evidence suggests it is the site of a weaving shed. Under the heading 'Cotton Spinners & Manufacturers', White's trade directory from 1837 listed 'Charles Ratcliffe (mfr) agent to Faulkener & Co'. The 1844 tithe apportionment for Settle named Charles Ratcliffe as owner-occupier of 'Cottages & garden' at the top end of the yard facing Albert Hill and of 'Weaving shops' at the lower end of the yard. The 1851 census return listed Mary Ann Ratcliffe, widow aged 23, sharing a house, probably in Chapel Square, with her baby daughter and Henry Hartley, her brother aged 21. She was entered as 'cotton manufacturer', he as 'manager of the above manufactory employing 5 men, 13 women, 3 boys and 4 girls'. From a lack of documentary evidence, they were not associated with any of Settle's other mills; the size of the workforce hints at a substantial enterprise. Charles and later Mary Ann's brother clearly operated what was listed in the tithe apportionment as the 'weaving shops' in Radcliffe Yard. The two rows of workers' cottages on what used to be called Back Lane (now Green Head Lane) below Radcliffe Yard – Higher and Lower Croft Streets – were not there in 1844 and were not separately listed in census returns prior to 1891.

To confuse the matter further, perhaps, the 1871 census made mention of a Thread Mill in Upper Settle.

T'owd Snuff photographed in 1990

The oldest part of the King's Mill complex on the Ribble, completely demolished when it was all converted to housing at the end of the last century, was T'owd Snuff, originally a snuff (tobacco) mill. In 1795 it was leased by John Proctor & Son who converted it to cotton manufacture. After a serious fire in 1837 it was rebuilt and extended but still relied on water power; this was *déjà vu* for Thomas Proctor whose Runley Bridge mill had burnt down just ten or so years earlier prompting him to lease Settle Mill (King's Mill's alternative name) from the Thornbers. The complex was extended in size on at least two occasions with two large multi-storey mill buildings, and converted to steam power.

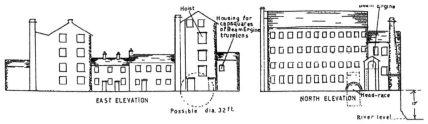

Kings Mill seen from the east (left) and from the north (right) (Jim Nelson, courtesy of Daniel Nelson)

Inset: Proctors Row at the bottom of Kirkgate: date-stone on a blocked-up cart arch with 'IP [John Proctor] 1833'

In 1856 a legal transaction between Thomas Proctor (jun.) and Ellin, his mother, concerned Thomas's King's Mill, a cotton mill erected by John and Thomas Proctor (sen.) near the site of a corn mill called Settle Mill along with houses, mill dam, Mill Island, and an enclosure called Mill Close. [55]

The King's Mill complex in 1993 when it was a storage depot for Langcliffe Paper Mill

The houses in question are Proctors Row, originally fourteen cottages but fifteen by 1851 when all but four were occupied by textile workers. Seventy-one people lived in the row then, of whom twenty-seven were either cotton weavers or spinners, or engaged in allied tasks.

In the 1850s Stephen Parkinson took on the mill, by 1881 a fresh partnership had it in hand, in 1896 it passed to one Barnes from Haslingden, then to Alan Wilkinson of Nelson in 1936: it had a chequered life. Closure came shortly before the outbreak of the Second World War. Its last working life was as a storage depot for Langcliffe paper mill until 1996 when it was sold for conversion to housing.

Bridge End Mill and cottages in 1995

The fifth of Settle's textile mills was the water-powered Bridge End Mill next to Settle Bridge. It was converted into a cotton spinning mill in 1785, 'newly erected' (presumably rebuilt) by 1801 [56] and taken by Edmund Armistead in 1802 but sold on as a cotton and worsted spinning mill in 1808 when he was bankrupted. William Clayton, who owned Langcliffe High Mill, bought it with its 4160 spindles, a large number given the size of the building, and a huge increase from the 300 of 1808. It was rebuilt, or remodelled, in 1818 by William Clayton who was also bankrupted, in 1849, after which Richard Bashall bought Clayton's mills though he leased Bridge End to Scott & Holden in 1852. In 1855, however, textile production ceased and it fell into a short period of disuse. The adjacent row of cottages bears the evidence of its probably having been back-to-back houses, though this is problematic: in 1841, 1851, 1861 and 1881 the censuses listed only five households, in 1891 six and in 1901 seven, with none annotated by the enumerators as 'uninhabited'. The 1871 returns, however, listed ten discrete dwellings which does suggest that they were built as back-to-backs. No. 6 may not have been a dwelling during the mill's textile life: In its east gable there are two large blocked openings, with a very high and wide blocked aperture at first-floor level suggesting non-residential use: this opening may have permitted a belt drive or other motive equipment connecting the main mill building with an ancillary workshop, but this is speculative.

An advertisement for Bridge End Mill in 1909 in its new guise.
The bell on the top was rung to call the textile workers to work

Bridge End Saw Mill in January 1940 (courtesy John Reid)

In 1861 mill owner Lorenzo Christie came up from Derbyshire to take on the Langcliffe mills including Bridge End, which latter he did not want. Bridge End was leased on a peppercorn rent to Henry Brassington, trading as Brassington Brothers & Corney, joiners, builders and contractors, who came up with Christie, and who ran it as water-powered saw mill and joinery workshop. The company name changed in 1916 to Brassington, Sons & Co. Ltd who operated, still using water power, until 1969. Among Brassingtons' many accomplishments is much of the furniture in St Alkelda's church in Giggleswick, restoration work on other Craven churches, and the building of Settle's War Memorial in 1925. When Brassingtons came to an end in November 1969 the building became an antiques repair workshop; in 1986 it was converted to flats. [57]

6

Faith

Holy Ascension Church

Until 1892 Settle was part of the ancient parish of Giggleswick so did not have its own parish church. The Church of the Holy Ascension was built to designs by Thomas Rickman, of Liverpool, in Early English style, or in the 'usual lancet style' with a wide nave and a spire-topped polygonal bell turret. [58] The building costs of £3000 were raised from public subscription, and it was consecrated in 1838. Unusually, it is aligned north-south rather than east-west. The first incumbent was the Rev'd Hogarth John Swale and on his retirement in 1842 he built Ingfield (now the Falcon Manor Hotel) as his retirement home. As was the norm in times past, many Anglican vicars saw themselves on a par socially with the landed gentry and lived accordingly. Because the incumbent of the parish church of St Alkelda in Giggleswick held the freehold to the land Holy Ascension was built on, an Act of Parliament of 1850 to sub-divide the ancient parish into several smaller parishes could not be implemented in his lifetime. [59] Thus, from 1838 to the death of the vicar of Giggleswick in 1892 Holy Ascension remained a Perpetual Curacy. Parochial separation came into being in that year.

Settle's earliest Christian place of worship was established by Quakers. John Kidd, who had a farm on Albert Hill, later the poor-house, and John Armistead sheltered early itinerant Quaker preachers and hosted illicit meetings in their houses. These early 'messengers' met with a mixed response but 'several inhabitants [of Settle] accepted their preaching' during 1652 and 1653. [60] In 1659 Howson's Croft on Kirkgate was bequeathed to the Quakers and in the following year two prominent Quakers bought land for a burial ground and Meeting House. Approval to build a formal Meeting House was forthcoming in 1678 but it only received a licence after the Act of Toleration of 1689 permitted worship outside the Established Church. The original meeting house was a very basic single-room structure.

Zion Chapel

In 1816 Zion Chapel was built above Castleberg Lane as an Independent Congregational chapel on land sold on favourable terms by John Birkbeck. Like Quakerism, the Independent movement arose out of visits by Itinerants, people who led a peripatetic life preaching and evangelising and were first seen in Settle in 1811; an outdoor evening meeting in 1813 is said to have attracted 1000 people. [61] Opened in 1817, for the first seven years services at Zion were run by students from Airedale Independent College in Idle, Bradford, who regularly journeyed to Settle to preach. The first minister was appointed in 1824, [62] though the first to live in the town was not appointed until 1855. [63] It was essentially kept going by the dedicated efforts of local people: one example was James Lambert, printer and stationer, who served as a deacon for twenty-six years; another, Titus Nelson, shoemaker, provided musical accompaniment to the hymns on his fiddle (see

Chapter 9). The Rev'd Benjamin Waugh (see Chapter 9) attended Sunday School here as a child. The chapel was renovated in 1874-75 and a school room/hall added in 1880. Sadly, declining numbers led to its closure in 2015.

Methodism in the Settle area can be traced back to Lawrence Batty of Newby Cote between Clapham and Ingleton; he encouraged Benjamin Ingham to come and preach here in 1743 and five years later he set up a Methodist society at his home. Other preachers visited the town from 1760. A room was rented in a house at the top of Kirkgate in 1771 and John Wesley preached in town in 1777 and 1784, in which latter year he stayed in the *Spread Eagle Inn*. In 1781 Edward Slater, one of Wesley's retinue, purchased a cottage and a 'parcel of ground whereon a chapel for divine worship is now erecting' in Chapel Street, a plot he owned until his death in 1808. [64]

Settle's first Wesleyan Chapel in Chapel Street (courtesy Museum of North Craven Life)

The Methodist trustees took Slater's chapel on, rebuilt it on a grander scale, calling it Bethesda, and opened it in 1810. During the previous year two members had rented a large room in The Folly to use as a Sunday School. Like Methodism in so many northern industrial communities, it boomed here. In 1879-80 a second plot of land with a cottage (and former smithy) was purchased on Chapel Square opposite, and a purpose-built school room was erected there in 1881 to cope with increased numbers. [65] This was used until 1939 and sold to the Freemasons in 1947 – since when it has been the Masonic Hall.

St John's Chapel prior to demolition in 2016 (courtesy Museum of North Craven Life)

In 1893 Bethesda Chapel was vacated and a new one built on Church Street; the old chapel was then used as the Parish Hall with workshops belonging to Salt's Mill in Saltaire on the upper floor. [66] Sadly, extensive structural issues led to the Church Street chapel being demolished in 2016, to be replaced by the St John's Terrace housing. The Chapel Street building had met the same fate, along with a whole complex of adjacent seventeenth-century cottages, in the mid 1960s to be replaced with what the planning authority of the day considered suitable architecture for a market town like Settle, namely what is now Delaney Court and the shops fronting the Chapel Street-High Street corner. The church hall for St John's was erected as a school room in 1939 and the new St John's came into use at the end of 2015 attached to the existing hall.

Settle's first Primitive Methodist chapel in Upper Settle

As time went on the Methodist Church as an institution fractured with one wing believing that Wesley's original philosophy and tenets were being undermined and weakened: thus began the 'working class' oriented Primitive Methodists. In

1841 Ebenezer Primitive Methodist Chapel was established on the corner of Victoria Street and Commercial Street, in what is now called Wapping Hall but formerly Wapping Room, in a building that had a meeting room above two small cottages.

Skipton Road Methodist Church in 1959. (Source: Jubilee Souvenir 1909 – 1959, courtesy Barbara Middleton)

Ebenezer was replaced when a larger and more suitable chapel was opened in 1909 at the corner of Skipton Road and High Hill Grove Street, called Skipton Road Methodist Church. This chapel remained within the Methodist fold but was bought in the mid to late 1970s by a small group of local worshippers under the auspices of the Assemblies of God. [67] This did not last long and the trustees decided to establish the independent Duke Street Pentecostal Church in 1979; it is now the Settle Christian Fellowship church.

Meanwhile, a legal agreement from 8 November 1915 between philanthropist John Robinson Esq. of Cragdale, Victoria Street, landlord, and the Anglican vicar and two churchwardens, granted the parish church use of Ebenezer Chapel and cottage beneath as a Mission Room at an annual rent of 5s. From 1937 to c. 1950 this was the home of the Pig Yard Club Museum, founded and run by Tot Lord (1899-1965), local cave explorer, cave archaeologist and luminary.

Upper Settle's Roman Catholic Church

Those of the Catholic faith first met in The Folly and later in Giggleswick but, eventually, a house connected with the Rope Walk in Upper Settle was purchased and a small chapel built, opening in 1864. [68] In 1883 this was totally rebuilt as a full-scale church (now converted to residential use), paid for by the first priest, Edward Woodhall. The priest from 1910-29 was Maximillianus Tillmann though in 1916 he was briefly interned because he was German born ... and assumed to be a spy or agent. He was given compensation and used this to purchase a plot of land near Bridge End in 1922. [69] In 1962 a new church hall was built on this plot and the old church was deconsecrated when a new church was built in 1974 on what is now called Tillman Close. In 1978 it was extended in size and the bell from the old church was installed here.

Finally in this brief survey of Settle's places of worship, Kingdom Hall of Jehovah's Witnesses at the south end of Craven Terrace was created by 1983 out of the Co-op shop which closed in 1979 (see photograph, page 40).

7

Education

In 1822 Settle had two schools including a ladies' boarding school; in 1834 three including a ladies' boarding and day school and Richard Pearson's school; in 1837 six 'academies' and the National School. However, the 1844 tithe apportionment listed only one plot as a school. This is not the whole story, though. The 1851 census returns listed two schoolmasters, five school mistresses, two pupil teachers (aged 15 and 17), one 'schoolmaster, pauper' aged only 37, and one private school mistress. Pupil teachers were promising individuals who showed above average ability and they were engaged on five-year apprenticeships before becoming fully qualified as teachers. [70] In 1861 Hannah Preston, aged 16, and William Lawler, aged 15, were recorded as pupil teachers (Edward Lawler, aged 28 – William's brother perhaps – was then the National School schoolmaster). William Moorby, aged 46, was the Infant School teacher and Thomas – his son, aged 16 – was a pupil teacher. In 1871 Richard Mason was a pupil teacher: there seems to have been a lack of continuity. In that year two National School schoolmistresses were listed: Sibylla Tennant, aged 23, and Eleanor Tennant, aged only 19.

The Terrace on Duke Street

The 1851 census returns showed that Isabella Henlock, who lived on The Terrace (Duke Street) in one of the three fine Greek Revival-style (George Webster of Kendal) villas that make up the row opposite FH Ellis's garage, ran a boarding school there. She had two live-in servants and seven boarding pupils on census day. In 1877 Sophia Towler ran a 'Ladies School' on New Road (now Station Road), assisted by her four daughters in looking after the educational needs of just two boarders; in the 1850s, though, there were seven pupil boarders. At one point in the late nineteenth century a private school for girls occupied Overdale on Skipton Road opposite Delaney Gardens. In 1901 Esther Pickard was the resident principal of Overdale Girls' Private School with five live-in school mistresses, five live-in servants and twenty boarding girls aged from eleven to seventeen.

The former National/Primary School on Castleberg Lane

The first National School was sited where Victoria Hall was later built; it was opened in 1816. Correctly speaking, there were two – one for girls and one for boys. In 1857 they were combined and re-sited on Castleberg Lane. In turn, this was closed down when the new primary school on Bond Lane was commissioned in 2002, linked to the construction of the adjacent supermarket. The fields here were purchased in 1930 from the Dawsons of Langcliffe Hall specifically to build a new primary school but funds only became available when the county council and school trustees/governors decided to sell part of the land to the supermarket company using the proceeds from this to build the new school.

Part of a gable wall, all that remains of the Mechanics Institute

In 1807 a large number of town worthies, including six Birkbecks, John Tatham and Alice Thornber, were instrumental in bringing to fruition the idea of a 'News Room and Library' by building a dedicated facility complete with a house for librarian William Bilton. [71] It was relatively short-lived, however, as the parties to the original indenture came together again to draw up a legal document concerning the building 'lately occupied as a Library and News Rooms [and] Librarian's House': it was to be converted into a dwelling and shop. [72] This was most likely because of developments initiated in 1831 which overtook this venture: one of the Birkbeck dynasty in Settle, George (1776-1841), had sought a very different path from his banker and merchant father by becoming a physician and professor. He was responsible for founding the nationwide Mechanics Institute movement, with one founded in Settle in 1831, designed to bring education and enlightenment to the working classes by offering lectures and evening classes and making available a reading room and library in return for a monthly subscription of 6d. For many years they convened their meetings in the Court House on New Road (Station Road) but by 1856 funds had been raised to erect a purpose-built 300-seat hall – the now-demolished Mechanics Hall – on Duke Street. [73] The hall was made available to other organisations, one of which was the local branch (or 'Tent') of the Independent Order of Rechabites, a large temperance Friendly Society. In 1857 the Institute helped set up the Settle Penny Bank, which may have been the one that was later based in the Town Hall. As time passed, the relevance of the Institute began to fade and in 1887 it was wound up. The building, however, stayed relevant to educating 'the masses' for far longer, hosting, for example, the Mechanics Club which itself folded in 1909, Settle Naturalist and Antiquarian Society from 1931 and Settle Museum until 1960. FH Ellis wanted to extend their car sales area so bought the building and demolished it in 1973 leaving only the stub gable wall in place. [74] The Mechanics Institute movement is fading from the public memory bank which is unfortunate given how widespread and transformative it was.

Settle also had a 'Commercial News Room' in the mid nineteenth century, stocking fifteen newspaper titles available on receipt of 1s. per day or 3s. quarterly. [75]

The entrance to the Adult Institute on Kirkgate

The obvious thirst for knowledge and self-improvement is further evidenced by the establishment in Settle in 1860 of an Adult School, part of the national Adult Schools Movement. Settle's was promoted by three local men – John and Richard Tatham and Ellwood Brocklebank, business partners on Cheapside, – and was housed in the Gallery Room of the Friends Meeting House. [76] It soon became known as the Settle (Adult) Institute which was accessed by an external staircase from Kirkgate/Spread Eagle Street. In 1872 a 'New School House' was built in the garden after which the Institute became the Reading Room and Library. By all accounts the Adult School was an instant success. [77]

Marshfield House

Charlotte Mason (1842-1923) was an inspired educator who believed that children's education should be grounded on a broad and liberal curriculum encouraging children to think (out of the box, I suppose we would say nowadays) rather than just being passive sponges soaking up endless facts. The *whole* person should be educated: 'Education is an atmosphere, a discipline, a life', she wrote. In 1891 she moved north and settled in Ambleside establishing a training school for governesses and child educators, which later became a teacher training college. In the following year her Parent's Educational Union added the word 'National' to its title and PNEU schools were set up across the country.

In 1943 a PNEU school was opened in Settle, initially in the (wooden) cricket club pavilion but later in Marshfield House. In 1967 it had thirty-two pupils aged 4-11, and was locally referred to as "Miss Smith's" (Una Smith was for a time the principal). [78] It closed in 1970. Through the 1990s the nursery section of Settle Primary School was housed in Marshfield until the new school opened in 2002.

It will be of interest to note in passing that Marshfield, built c. 1750, was occupied for a time by Countess Gyllenborg, daughter of a Swedish Prime Minister, who died here in 1766. Her daughter stayed on until 1772. It was burnt down a few years later and rebuilt in its present form as the residence of a succession of gentry occupants until purchased in 1826 by the Rev'd Richard Dawson of Halton Gill, Littondale, for his two daughters.

The secondary school serving Settle and the whole surrounding area is across the river in Giggleswick. Founded in 1907 as Settle Girls' High School, it became the co-educational, comprehensive Settle High School half a century later. [79] In 2004 it became Settle College.

8

Hospitality

As the manor court system declined in importance in favour of go-ahead tenant farmers and tradesmen, the economic basis of the town began to change. Settle looked more to trade and artisanship, drawing in increasing numbers of people who needed somewhere to stay and eat. Out of this grew the town's early inns. As trade continued to expand more attention was paid to the appalling road system and, while road maintenance was the responsibility of each township, it clearly made sense for local people to keep them in good order. With the growth of the post-road network from 1667, connecting post-towns, and with considerable improvements to that system after 1700, Settle became ever more accessible as it lay on the post-road from York to Lancaster. We do not have the names of Settle's earliest inns but we do know who the innholders were: a case from 1594, recorded in the Settle manor court rolls, involved Adam and Jenet Pailey of Settle. In 1595 an innholder called Baxter was involved in a court case. Fast forward another half century or so, when Settle's inns had become more market orientated, we do have inn names: we will return to these shortly.

As the centuries passed a hierarchy of 'hostelries' emerged. [80] Ten inns are known to have existed in Settle at one time or another (for example, seven in 1822 and eight in 1840) and several pubs and beer-houses. Between 1789 and 1843 four stage coach services broke their journeys in Settle including the 'Diligence', the 'True Briton' and the 'Kendal Union'. In the early decades of the twentieth century Settle had four breweries: Bentleys behind the *Talbot Hotel*, Dutton's behind the *King William*, the Lion Brewery behind *Ashfield* and Massey's behind the *Golden Lion*. [81] In the nineteenth century twenty-two wagon-carriers were based in Settle, of which fifteen used an inn as their key staging post. In addition, as we saw earlier, until well into the twentieth century, Settle hosted regular livestock fairs and a produce market drawing in untold numbers of potential customers.

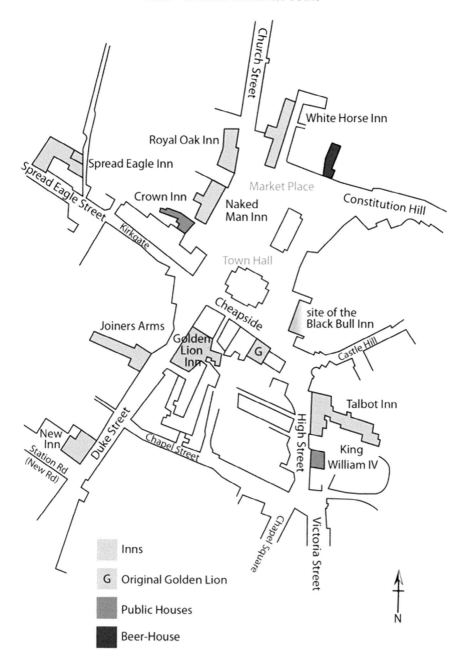

Map 5: Licensed premises in Settle, past and present

In 1771 Settle had fifteen licensed premises, in 1803 nine, from 1822-28 eight, from 1834-57 eleven, and by 1904 five – two listed as 'hotels' and three as 'public houses'. [82] All the West Riding Quarter Sessions records named the licensee, few the establishment. For 1793-98 both in a very limited way are available: Settle's 'principal inns' then were William Fawcett's *Golden Lion* and William Bradley's *Spread Eagle* (Map 5). A sobering statistic is that only nine 'visitors' were listed as resident overnight on census day in 1851 across all of Settle's inns: this may be because the census was taken on 30 March which did not coincide with any markets or fairs and was rather early in the trading season.

The Naked Man in the late nineteenth century

The will of John Cookeson of Settle, yeoman, dated 28 August 1690, itemised his possessions in the *Naked Man* room by room: 'Red Chamber, Middle Chamber, Chamber over house, old Chambers, Kitching Loft, Low Parlor, higher Parlor, butterie, Cellar, Bodistead' and two barns. In all there were twenty-eight beds, five chamber pots, five tankards, eleven pans, umpteen pairs of sheets, blankets, coverlets, bolsters and thirty-four chairs and stools. Beyond any doubt this was an inn at that time. The date-stone bears the inscription 'IC 1663' … and, by the way, has nothing to do with nakedness.

The will of Robert Cookson, also a yeoman, dated 9 June 1702, listed 'Sun Chamber, Higher Chamber over the Parlor, Higher Chamber over the House, High Porch Chamber, Out Chamber over the Shopp, Parlor Chamber, Chamber over the house, Porch Chamber, Staire Case, bodystead, Parlor, Celler, Brewhouse, Stable, barne'. In the cellar were two large brewing pans, two large gelkers (tubs used in the early stages of ale/beer making), three tearses (casks), four barrels, and one hogs head. This was not just an inn: it was a substantial and busy inn.

In 1828 this inn was named along with sixteen other premises in Settle in the West Riding Quarter Sessions list of alehouse keepers, and a legal document from 2 October 1832 referred to a dwelling house 'occupied as an Inn' called the *Naked Man*. The Settle Chronicle described it, on 1 March 1858, as 'the best adapted inn in the town, with a grocer's shop at the "New End"' – the section that is clearly newer at the front than the original inn building.

Amongst other roles, the *Naked Man* acted as the staging post for carriers to Kendal (on Tuesdays, by J. Wrathall), to Bentham and Lancaster (Mondays and Thursdays, Thomas Charnley and Thomas Bentham), to Lancaster only (Mondays and Thursdays, by Sedgwick's Waggons), to Austwick (Tuesdays, W. Lord), to Stainforth (Tuesdays and Saturdays, George Lund), and to Ingleton (also Tuesdays, James Foster).

As this late nineteenth-century photograph (above) shows, it changed its identity from inn to hotel; it lost its licence in 1917. By 1929 it had become Ye Olde Naked Man Café.

The Golden Lion, probably in the late nineteenth century (Museum of North Craven Life)

It has been repeatedly written that the owner of the *Golden Lion* relocated the inn from Cheapside to Duke Street when the turnpike road was realigned to enter Settle along Duke Street in 1753. This is simply not true: the inn had already been moved to Duke Street by 1749. Two indentures prove this beyond doubt as both stated unambiguously that it stood on what was in that year still called Duck Street. [83] It may be that this inn was one of those mentioned in the 1590s but this has not been proven. One fact is proven, though: the original main door to the Cheapside premises, now hidden from external view by a very recent addition, bears a date-stone '1697' with the initials of John Robinson, the then innholder. The present inn has a date-stone '1671' above the north doorway: this refers to the farmhouse that stood here prior to its becoming an inn. By the late nineteenth century its proprietors were advertising the *Golden Lion* as a hotel that hosted the nobility, gentry and even royalty (1888 advertisement) or as a 'High-class Family & Commercial' Hotel (1897 advertisement). An advertisement from 1933 described it as 'Famous since 1760' and the 'Premier Hotel of the District' with parking for 'up to 30 cars'. [84]

The former White Horse

The former prominent Settle inn, the *White Horse*, opposite the *Royal Oak*, is known from at least 1724 when the probate inventory of John Lawson, its owner, itemised 17 beds, 17 plates, 14 pewter dishes, 20 napkins and 24 blankets but only 3 (pewter) chamber pots, as well as 20 casks of ale each holding 100 gallons of ale in the cellar valued at £5 17s. 6d. It was no mean inn. Rooms were named as 'Garrett, chamber over parlour, Sun Garrett, Garrett over the porch, porch chamber, Chamber over House, Chamber parlour, Chamber over shop, and house'[body]. There was a brewhouse, barn, garden and attached croft. The date-stone 'RP L 1671' probably refers to an earlier Lawson. An indenture from 1735 added to its list of appurtenances 'backsides', in other words a yard at the rear. In the 1740s it was run as an inn by Izat Bell and Jane Hargraves, both widows, though it was still owned by Lawson; [85] in 1806 John Green occupied it. An indenture of 1834 noted that Helen Bowskill, widow of the previous innholder John, was herself the occupant; and it further noted that the inn had recently been rebuilt. In the following year Thomas Bowskill, cattle dealer, and William Bowskill, innkeeper, were involved in the inn and what is now called Howson's Yard. [86]

In 1888 a local almanac advertised that Henry Wilson, publican, offered 'well-aired beds ... good stabling ... and a horse and trap for hire'. It was also the stage terminus for carriers to destinations around Ingleborough on Tuesdays and Fridays. The White Horse was advertised as the *White Horse Hotel* in 1913, but as the *White Horse* PH in a 1928 trade directory. It closed in the 1940s.

The former Spread Eagle Inn

The *Spread Eagle Inn*, at one time simply the *Eagle* according to indentures from 1836, occupied most of the area either side of Spread Eagle Street where modern Kirkgate opens out just east of Victoria Hall. Its coach house, for example, was where the northern entrance to Ashfield car park is. From 1807-43 it was the overnight stop for the Leeds-Kendal 'Kendal Union' stage coach, initially three days a week, latterly daily. The Hon. John Byng, on his grand tour, stayed here in 1792 arriving on a 'dismal, black, raining day' and finding Settle a 'poor gloomy place'. William Bradley was the landlord and he cannot have been pleased with Byng's assessment of the inn: he spent his nights in a 'bad and dismal inn, with mice running about' in 'the worst inn's worst room'. When one considers what he had dined on he must be considered more than a little harsh in that judgement as he made no derogatory comments about the meals: his 'early dinner' consisting of beef steak, lamb chops, pickled salmon and tart set him back the princely sum of 9d.; while his first night's supper was lamb chops, potted trout and tart, again all for 9d. [87] From 1793-98 the *Spread Eagle* was listed in a directory as one of the town's two principal inns, with Bradley in charge. Thomas Procter, sculptor and painter, was born here in 1753 but suffered a miserable end in London in 1794. His father, Robert, had opened the *Spread Eagle* as an inn, after renovating an earlier structure in 1734, running it as owner/innholder with his wife Ellen.

In June 1850 the inn was put up for auction on the death of Robert Atkinson who owned or ran it, with its 'spacious yard' and stabling behind the inn, shippons, brewhouse, coach house and a barn which is currently a garden shop. Settle's Tuesday markets and alternate Monday cattle fairs were given prominence as reasons to purchase the inn. The *Spread Eagle* closed in 1852.

The former Joiners Arms Inn

Commercial Yard, off Duke Street in Settle, perpetuates the name of what in 1913 was the *Commercial Hotel*. The tall buildings that line Commercial Yard were stables, coach (or trap) house, ostlers' accommodation and part of what for more than a century was the *Joiners Arms*, yet another of the town's many inns. An indenture and mortgage, from 1779, with William Willman, innholder, as one of the parties involved, concerned his 'new erected [house] now used as an Inn' called the Joiners Arms, complete with barn, two stables, brewhouse, a room over the brewhouse, warehouse, garden, orchard and the usual 'backside'. [88]

The 1774 datestone over the arch giving access to the yard from Duke Street confirms this 'new' build. He died in 1815, still the innholder, and William Tate took on the mantle after his death. *The Joiners* was the staging post for a weekly wagon service to Grassington via Airton and to Tosside, at least during the middle part of the nineteenth century; from 1816-43 for the 'True Briton' coach it was a calling point on its journeys three days a week between Kendal and Leeds. In 1851 John Preston was the innkeeper but by 1857 Robert Atkinson was listed as 'victualler' here. The precise date when the *Joiners* became the *Commercial* has not been identified, but a trade directory for 1867 listed it as the *Commercial Hotel* and one for 1908 as the *Commercial Temperance Hotel*.

The former New Inn

At the corner of Station Road and Duke Street the building with a curving façade and an ornate doorway on the west side was the *New Inn*. It is recorded as an inn from at least June 1736 according to the probate inventory of John Redmayn 'of Newinn'. [89] In 1814 innholder E. Moorhouse charged a customer 17s. for dinner, drinks and horses' hay, which compared favourably with another bill, from March 1812, when the same cost £1 6s. 4½d. According to the writer Howson, in 1850 this was one of Settle's two main inns, having knocked the *Spread Eagle* off its pedestal. [90] It was run by widow Margaret Gifford. As with other inns here, the New Inn was in partnership with carriers who connected Settle with Clitheroe on Thursdays and Colne on Saturdays in the early to mid nineteenth century, when it was owned by the wealthy Birkbeck family. It was still operational as a public house in 1904 but a trade directory for 1908 referred to it as other types of buildings. When New Road (Station Road) was created by the railway company in 1849 the inn lost its long narrow yard and ancillary buildings on both sides; some of these buildings had been erected little more than a decade earlier. [91]

The Royal Oak, mid twentieth century (Horner Collection)

The *Royal Oak* is recorded as an inn from 1689 – it has a date-stone 1686 – and was rebuilt or substantially reworked in 1720 and 1802. An indication of its popularity is given in the probate inventory of Francis Bell, innkeeper, in 1743 when the cellar contained fourteen barrels of ale and the inn had three ground floor rooms, two first floor chambers and three garret rooms up in the roof space. [92] Joseph Bell is recorded as occupant from 1757-87 at which point it was demised to Rowland Atkinson; in 1836 Robert Atkinson was the innkeeper, in 1851 Henry Ayrton.

The *Talbot Inn* looks to be a purpose-built inn, complete with yard and a range of outbuildings – formerly barn, stables, brewhouse and 'staff' accommodation – dating to the late eighteenth century. A series of indentures, from 1825-37, show that it changed hands on a number of occasions, from William Oldfield to his widow Mary in 1825, to William Howard in 1832, to John Clapham from 1833-37. [93] Anecdotal evidence suggests it was the preferred meeting place for leather workers and traders, possibly owing to its close proximity to Settle's two tanneries.

The *Black Bull Inn* no longer exists and it is not possible to state with conviction exactly on which plot it was sited. It has rather a shadowy history and has not been found in trade directories and was not listed in the 1828 Quarter Sessions list of innholders. Its existence is, however, recorded in legal indentures: in 1751, 1753 and 1755, for example, Thomas Capstacke was the innholder, though not the owner, and the premises included stables, brewhouse and other outbuildings so it was definitely an inn rather than just a public house. A later indenture, from 1826, is telling: the document clearly states '... formerly used as an Inn and called and known by the name of the Black Bull ...' Exactly when it went out of business is also not known but it cannot have been much before 1826. [94] The range of buildings was demolished c. 1870.

SETTLE.

MR. CHARLES E. TOWLER

WILL

OFFER FOR SALE BY AUCTION,

AT THE

CROWN HOTEL, SETTLE,

On Tuesday, the 19th May, 1891,

At 2·30 p.m., precisely and subject to Conditions of Sale,

THE FULLY LICENSED PUBLIC HOUSE,

KNOWN AS

The "Crown Hotel," Settle,

COMPRISING :

Bar, Bar Parlour, Front Parlour, Smoke Room, Two Large Kitchens, Four Good Cellars, Upstairs Sitting-Room, Three Bedrooms, Large Room over Kitchen, Bath Room, W.C., and Large Attic, as now in the occupation of Mr. Robert Batty.

The Property is leasehold for a long term of years, and subject to the payment of a yearly ground rent of 4/6.

The Hotel faces the Market Place, in Settle, and, being well tenanted and much frequented by excursionists, affords a favourable investment to Brewers and Capitalists.

For further information apply to

WRIGHT, CHARLESWORTH & Co.,

SOLICITORS,

SETTLE AND SKIPTON.

Sales advertisement for the former Crown in 1891

In 1835, according to an indenture, *The Board* was occupied by John Holroyd and his tenants, with the text focussed on a 'Dwellinghouse Dramhouse liquor cellary and vaults' which had hitherto 'formerly [been] occupied as a public house and Dramshop' called the *Board*. In that year it had recently been demolished and rebuilt in its present form as 'dramshop and vaults'. [95] From details within the indenture, this can only have been what later was called the *Crown Inn*, listed as such in a trade directory of 1867 and an indenture of 1879 by which 'Henry Holden of Settle, spirit merchant' sold to Edmund Crabtree the 'inn called the Crown Inn'. Use of the term 'inn' was a misnomer according to the 1835 description: a dram shop was a bar or retail shop selling alcohol in small measures, while the word vaults was used for the room within a pub that was set aside to serve working class men – men, not men and women. In other words, at least in 1835 it was no more than a lowly pub.

Various Acts were passed in the first half of the nineteenth century. Rationalisation of all existing legislation was the purpose of the 1822 Licensing Act and the Alehouse Act 1828, but the Beer Act 1830 liberalised the brewing and selling of beer partly, perhaps, as the desperate attempt of a very unpopular government to curry favour among the (male) voting masses. One immediate impact of this law was a mushrooming in the number of beer-houses (for in-house consumption) and beer-shops (for take-aways), as the only condition imposed was that anyone paying the requisite licence fee could turn their own house into a beer-house/-shop as long as they erected a board outside with their own name. For this reason, especially in the North of England, countless beer-houses became known as *The Board*, though this name seems to have first appeared after the passing of the 1822 Act. Many quite soon either went out of business or became public houses adopting a more personalised name. The *Crown* was called *The Board* up to 1835. It was not uncommon to add the word 'inn' to a pub name as a sales ploy. Having said this, the 1851 census listed James Lund as 'innkeeper and farmer' with a live-in servant and ostler as well as his wife: sixteen-year old ostler James Ellison's role was to look after guest's horses as stableboy and groom.

In an advertisement in 1887 licensee Robert Batty offered potential customers 'good stabling' and a Sales Notice of 1891 announced the impending auction of 'The Crown Hotel' – had Batty fallen on hard times? This was not its end, though, as in 1909 it was operating as a carrier station. It shut down either in 1914 or 1917, became a lodging house and was later refronted and made into a shop.

The former King William IV public house

Another unintended consequence of the 1820s Beer Acts was the number of beer-houses that eventually took the name *King William IV* – it was enacted in that king's reign and for this reason his popularity ratings soared among dedicated drinkers. The tithe apportionment map of 1844 marked it as a beer-shop. Through its twentieth-century life it was a public house.

There was another public house of which little is known: the 1871 census listed a dwelling on Victoria or Albert Street as formerly 'the Sun Public House'.

The Temperance Hotel on the north-east corner of Market Place,
drawn by John Dawson Watson 1853 (courtesy Museum of North Craven Life)

The former Temperance Hotel behind The Shambles

Another inevitable consequence of the 1820s Beer Acts which deregulated public houses and the whole business of consuming alcohol was a surge in drunkenness rates and misery caused by men drinking their way through much of their meagre weekly wage. In turn, a consequence of this was the inception and rapid growth of the anti-alcohol Temperance Movement: Bands of Hope (from 1847), the Rechabites (from 1835) and local Temperance Societies railed against alcohol and urged their followers to sign the teetotal pledge. A society was formed in Settle in 1834 and within four years 350 people had signed and by 1844 420. [96] Temperance hotels also sprang up in the mid nineteenth century providing an alternative to inns. Apart from the *Commercial Temperance Hotel* on Duke Street, there were several others that came and went. At the end of nineteenth century Ashfield was a temperance hotel though decades later the *Ashfield Hotel* was given a licence.

At least in the 1850s there was a *Temperance Hotel* at the bottom of Constitution Hill (shown in the image above) opposite the modern Co-op, and *Castlebergh Hotel* was a temperance hotel in the twentieth century but long since demolished: it stood on the present Co-op site.

9

People

In 1851 there were 1786 people – men, women and children – resident overnight on census day, living in 380 individual dwellings within the town. This contrasts with 2564 across the whole parish on census night in 2011, not a huge increase over 160 years. It also contrasts with 1153 in 1811 and 1508 in 1821. [97] This chapter provides brief biographies of a selection of Settle's residents over time: the choice has been hard to make but it does not ignore 'lowly' folk in favour of their 'betters'. They are presented here in strict alphabetical order.

The selection is regrettably, and inevitably perhaps, dominated by men but women do appear in the record. We have already met Alice Thornber who was clearly a redoubtable and business-minded individual. As far back as the late seventeenth century Elizabeth Skirrow ran a general shop in town and when she died in 1714 her probate inventory was impressive in its long list of items. For some reason, Alphonsine Jarry (1822-1912) settled here in the 1850s with her sister and a substantial inheritance from her father; at the time of her demise she lived at Fernhill on Constitution Hill. For four decades she helped with the church and Sunday School and on her death much of her estate was bequeathed to the Rev'd John Robinson Charity for the 'benefit of the aged and infirm of the parish of Giggleswick'. [98] It should also be remembered that it was common here, as everywhere, for widows to run inns and pubs as long as they were 'of honest conversation' (not gossips or loud mouths).

Memorial to Dr William Birkbeck (1776-1841) in St Alkelda's Church, Giggleswick (photo by the author with thanks to the Priest-in-Charge)

The Birkbecks were a remarkable family, a dynasty even, whose collective achievements illustrate social mobility par excellence. They originated in Mallerstang as yeoman farmers but William (1675-1751) moved to Settle in 1698, established himself as a general dealer, becoming a prominent Quaker. In time his business grew into that of wool stapler, one who bought wool, graded it by quality and sold it on to manufacturers, and his wealth (and, no doubt, his Faith) led him to give loans which is ultimately how the family bank started (see Chapter 4). The interest in textiles later on led to the Birkbecks taking on a watermill in Giggleswick for conversion to cotton spinning, as well as Linton Mill on the Wharfe and Low Mill, Addingham. Their names crop up time and again in business dealings in Settle, and they owned properties on Duke Street, Cheapside and elsewhere. William (1772-1838) built Ashfield as his home (see Chapter 10). His brother George (1776-1841) took a path away from business by training as a doctor and later founding the Mechanics Institute movement and Birkbeck College in London (see Chapter 7). John Birkbeck (III, 1781-1844) built Anley House overlooking the Ribble (see Chapter 10). John Birkbeck (IV, 1817-90 and V, 1842-92) were keen Alpinists with John III a founder member of the Alpine Club. [99] The last of the family to have an interest in Anley House died in 1976 though the rump of Anley Estate (but not Anley House) is still part-owned by a Birkbeck. [100]

Leonard Bolland (1669-1712) was an apothecary (someone who prepared and sold medicines) and a landowner, as was his son Christopher. [101] In 1692 Leonard purchased the *Golden Lion Inn*. The family clearly prospered, as evidenced by entries in the 1844 tithe apportionment and 1851 census: Margaret Bolland, unmarried, owned and let out two houses, four fields and a plantation in addition to owning and living at Town Head (see Chapter 10) and owning Castleberg Plantation. In 1851 she shared that house with three female relatives and five live-in servants.

The Bowskills were a prolific family of traders and craftsmen. We have already met John, blacksmith, in 1767 (see Chapter 4); in 1803 John and William were both blacksmiths, William was a master blacksmith at least between 1834 and 1851; in 1834 John was a horse dealer and Thomas a cattle dealer. Their memory is preserved in Bowskills Yard.

The one-time home and surgery of Dr Charles Buck in Market Place

Settle-born Dr Charles W. Buck (1851-1932) qualified as a surgeon in 1875 and practised as a doctor in Settle until retirement in 1916, with both home and surgery in Market Place. A friend of the composer Edward Elgar, Buck was a musician in his own right and conductor of Settle's String Band and Amateur Operatic Society. He spent most of his retirement in a house at the bottom of Belle Hill in Giggleswick.

John Delaney in later life

John Delaney's story is truly one of rags to riches. Said to have been born to a large Irish family in 1846 or, according to another story, in Stalybridge, his early life journey brought him to work in the cotton mill in Langcliffe, later also to run what was to become a very early co-operative shop. By 1881 he was also a coal merchant and by 1891 was living in Craven Terrace in Settle described as a 'stone quarry owner and coal merchant'. In the 1870s he borrowed money from a Quaker banker to buy a horse and cart and was soon at Manchester studying for a degree in geology, and this must have been one factor that launched him into the quarrying of limestone, owning quarries at Horton in Ribblesdale, Threshfield and Broughton. [102] In 1910 he became a Justice of the Peace and entered local politics. He bought a large plot of land at Halsteads on Skipton Road on the then southern edge of town, building among other properties a large house for himself. He started with nothing; he died a very rich and respected man.

Portrait of John Coakley Lettsom (© and courtesy The Medical Society of London)

We met John Coakley Lettsom (1744-1815) earlier (see Map 3): his life, too, was out of the ordinary. His Quaker father was a plantation (and slave) owner on the tiny island of Tortola in the West Indies. The family had seven sets of male twins: only the final pair survived infancy, including John who was sent to England at the tender age of six, first to Liverpool and then to live with a Quaker in Warrington whose brother was a London doctor. John clearly took to the profession and was apprenticed for five years to the Quaker surgeon and apothecary Abraham Sutcliffe in Settle with whom he lodged. He moved to London in 1766 and in 1773 founded The Medical Society of London whose headquarters are in Lettsom House on Chandos Street. Lettsom is remembered as human rights campaigner, abolitionist, mineralogist and botanist as well as a doctor and Quaker. He only spent five years in Settle but this episode made him what he was to become in later life.

REMOVAL OF BUSINESS.

TITUS NELSON

Has the pleasure to announce that he has entered upon the Shop lately occupied by Mr Mason, Duke Street, where he will keep a select assortment of

BOOTS & SHOES,

Of the best quality, and hopes to be favoured with the custom of those who are desirous of being well and promptly served. Especial attention will be paid to the Bespoke business, Repairs neatly executed.
An assortment of French Goods including Ladies' House Boots, French Slippers. &c. &c., just to hand.

Duke Street, Settle, Nov. 12th, 1855.

An advertisement for Titus Nelson's business in Settle, 1855 (Craven Herald)

Titus Nelson, in 1847 and at the age of 24, a third-generation boot and shoe maker, left his home in Cononley, south of Skipton, to make a new life in Settle. The town's importance as a tanning and leather centre was clearly a major draw and the opportunities are illustrated by the fact that Settle already had six established boot and shoe makers. By 1861 he was described as a master shoemaker and, from an advertisement in 1865, was making 'bespoke boots and shoes' and 'French Goods' (ladies' shoes and slippers). Since 1865 he has ensconced in the premises still occupied by his direct descendant – the seventh generation of bespoke boot and shoe makers in the family and the fifth based in Settle.

*An invoice from Christopher Ralph's business,
1896 (author's collection)*

We have encountered the Proctor mill-owning family, and the Thornbers, already and their place in Settle's economy and society must be kept in mind, as must that of the Ralph family. Like the Proctors, the Thornbers, the Bowskills and the Nelsons, the Ralphs were not high-born but they made a real contribution to the prosperity of the area. In 1851 eleven households were headed by Ralph men, all born in Settle and most living in Upper Settle. Their census entries shed light on how members of Victorian families spanned the social and economic spectrum. In that year Thomas was a master carpenter; Robert, another Thomas, and James were all journeymen (joiner, blacksmith and stonemason respectively), meaning they were fully trained but worked for someone else. John and William worked in a cotton mill so at least had a regular wage. Yet another William was further down the scale working as a farm labourer, as was another Robert, doing what was an incredibly common job for young rural-based men. At the bottom of the scale were Luke, a mason's labourer but in 1851 a pauper, and Matthew and Samuel, both farm labourers and also paupers.

Later in the nineteenth century William Ralph, of Victoria Street, leased and worked Combs Quarry at Helwith Bridge producing a wide range of 'Blue Flag' products. In turn, his son Christopher, born in 1858, continued what was a very successful business into the twentieth century, and their products can be seen far and wide including water tanks, cisterns, dairy slabs, porch roofing and footbridge slabs. [103]

*Sutcliffe House on the corner of Duke Street and Cheapside.
Note the original ornate house door*

As we saw earlier, in the 1760s John Lettsom stayed with Abraham Sutcliffe in this house, built (or rebuilt) by Sutcliffe c. 1750. Sutcliffe was born in York in 1721 but became an errand boy for a surgeon in Kendal; he clearly felt drawn to that profession and taught himself Latin and each winter for some years he *walked* the 145 miles (230km) from Kendal to Edinburgh, and back, to attend medical classes; he later came to live in Settle. Like so many prominent Settle residents he was a Quaker; he set himself up here as an apothecary c. 1740 and true to Quaker philosophy he held the interests of others very much to the fore, for example by employing a succession of apprentices such as Lettsom. In 1786 he retired to Sheffield where he died in 1798; [104] his business and practice in Settle were left to his son William (1759-1840). [105] The tithe apportionment of 1844 recorded Jane Sutcliffe as owner of the house though it was occupied by Francis Ellis and Thomas Dixon Burrow as 'Bank Houses etc'.

On the frontage of what used to be a bank (see page 38) there is a tablet, unveiled in 1927, in memory of the Rev'd Benjamin Waugh (1839-1908). He was born on this site in an earlier building which served as dwelling and saddlery for his father and family. His mother died when he was nine and he was sent away to stay with an uncle in Warwickshire where he attended school. In 1862 he entered the church and was ordained as a Congregational minister in Greenwich in 1867. He was a philanthropist, lobbyist and avid campaigner for the improvement of children's welfare. In 1884 he was instrumental in founding the London Society for the Prevention of Cruelty to Children which became National (NSPCC) in 1889, in which year his campaign against child cruelty was formalised in the Children's Charter.

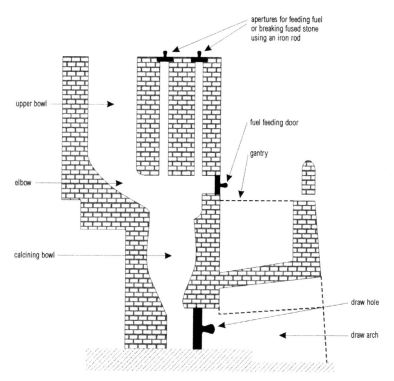

*A 12m-high lime kiln design patented by
John Winskill junior, 1889 (© the author)*

John Winskill was born in Kirkby Lonsdale in 1815 or 1817 and established a business in Settle in 1850, initially living in Back Stables (Yard). He was a master stonemason and within a year employed twenty-five men and had a live-in apprentice, 24-year old John Buller from Slaidburn. In 1871 he lived on Victoria Street, with two live-in apprentices, as well as in 1881, by which time he had thirty in his employ. His business involved making headstones, building, general contracting and, from before 1871, farming 135 acres (54 hectares). He died on 22 May 1890 and an obituary noted that he was 'held in high esteem. Many of the houses and public buildings erected in the Settle district during the last 40 years have been reared under Mr Winskills direction'. He was a Poor Law Guardian and a Rechabite. [106] His son, also John, born in 1862, carried on the family business. Both appeared regularly in trade directories but there was no mention in any of them, or in their advertisements in local household almanacs or, indeed, in John senior's obituary, of another remarkable achievement that both shared. In 1872 John the father patented a revolutionary design for a lime kiln that stood 13.5m high and in 1889 his son patented an improvement on that design. [107]

Collecting water at 'Slippy Slops' (Riley Collection)

Having highlighted a number of individuals, across the social classes, it seems appropriate to end this chapter with a well-known spot in Settle – officially Well Steps but affectionately Slippy Slops. Apart from the pub and the chapel, this was probably the most important place in Settle for ordinary working people and their families. This was not just somewhere to get water, to do the weekly wash or for the blacksmith to take horses to water but, crucially, it was where folk would gather to exchange news and gossip, to catch up on the latest scandal and giggle over someone's mishap.

10

Buildings

In this chapter a variety of buildings, some not introduced earlier, will be brought into the story along with personages relevant to the whole story. As with People, this (alphabetical) selection cuts across status, size and original function. We have encountered the Birkbecks in several contexts and the first two buildings arguably illustrate the height of their social and economic rise.

Anley House, 1993

Anley House, overlooking the Ribble to the south of the town (historically never called Anley Hall) was built in 1818 for John Birkbeck (III, 1781-1844). A banker, he clearly aspired to gentry status by building a house on this scale. Newly widowed in 1844, his widow, Margaret, was listed on the tithe apportionment as head of household and, in 1851, with daughter, son-in-law and eight live-in servants. In 1871 her son, John (IV, 1817-90), was head of household with ten live-in servants; by 1891 that number had been halved – perhaps reality was beginning to take hold.

A Stansfeld family group in the garden of Ashfield in the 1860s (Riley Collection)

The fine building standing on the west side of Duke Street – Ashfield – was described by Pevsner as a 'dignified Late Georgian building of five bays ... with a semicircular porch on Tuscan columns'. [108] It was built for William Birkbeck (1772-1838) in the 1830s, again stressing the family's claim to gentry status. The main staircase is rightly described as 'grand' and the scale of the gardens once attached to the house was impressive. The whole of Ashfield car park, the bowling green, the vets' property and everything up to Bond Lane (prior to the coming of the railway) was part of the grounds. Rose Cottage, on the corner of Station Road and Bond Lane, was the main gate lodge into the grounds. Various legal documents from the mid nineteenth century refer not just to gardens but to a 'pleasure ground'. [109] On the section of the car park nearest to the later railway viaduct there was a large plant nursery, cleared away in the 1930s. William was not to enjoy his crowning glory for long, though, as he died within a few years of the house being completed; the 1844 tithe apportionment listed Rachael Birkbeck as owner-occupier. In 1834 one of William's daughters, Sarah, married George Stansfeld (1803-69), a partner in the Craven Bank (there was also intermarriage between Stansfelds and John Birkbeck of Anley House). [110] The family group shown in this image from the 1860s comprises George, Sarah and some of their children. A further marital link brought together another local branch of the Birkbecks – John of Bankwell, Giggleswick, married his cousin Rachel Stansfeld in 1867. Meanwhile, in 1865, Sarah Stansfeld had married Charles Henry Charlesworth of Holly Bank, Giggleswick, solicitor: by 1877 he was listed as head of household at Ashfield. [111] The building has been through a variety of roles – temperance hotel and (licensed) hotel, and now Social Club.

Through the nineteenth and early twentieth century many family fortunes waned as priorities and social attitudes changed, leading to would-be statements of grandeur reduced in status. Anley and Ashfield are two local cameos that prove the point. The former grand houses of Whitefriars and Marshfield are two others.

The former Assembly Rooms

The old Craven Assembly Rooms in Bishopdale Court are well hidden but they can be seen from the narrow ginnel (Roger Lane on Lettsom's map) that connects Kirkgate with Whitefriars car park. The frontage has been so altered as to be virtually unrecognisable and the rear part of the building might leave one wondering how it was ever allowed to be constructed in the first place. Certainly, it cannot be described as attractive or aesthetically pleasing. After 1945 part of it was used as a workshop by Salts of Saltaire's worsted mill.

The first court house and police station on Station Road

On the north side of Station Road (formerly New Street/Road) the rather grand building with the external staircase was Settle's old Court House; the adjoining building, with prominent stone window surrounds and altered doorway, was the first police station. Ordnance Survey six-inch mapping from 1847 depicted the court house but not the police station. The old system of locally-appointed constables came to an end with the building of the police station in 1857.

Cragdale on Duke Street

In much the same way as Ashfield, Marshfield, Whitefriars and Anley, Cragdale was built as a residence and statement of social status, c. 1830 by John Peart. He was a solicitor and co-founder of the Craven Bank in 1791. To enable this, he had an existing farmhouse and cottages demolished. [112] Cragdale retained its large gardens, extending back to what is now Greenfoot car park, into the twentieth century but, like all the other 'big' houses, it slid down the social scale eventually housing a tea room and later becoming the police station, with a new Court House tagged on to its southern end. It is now dwellings.

The Drill Hall

At the foot of Castleberg stands a rather severe and austere building first erected as a Drill Hall. It was conceived and funded by Walter Morrison of Malham Tarn House, Lt Col in the West Riding Rifle Volunteers, in 1864, following on from the Volunteer Act 1863 and therefore one of the earliest such drill halls in the country. It served as a place where the Settle Volunteer Corps could meet, drill, practise and store their equipment; the armoury is thought to have been in the basement. For live practice they already had the Attermire Range, erected in 1860 on the south side of Warrendale Knotts. The Corps was disbanded in 1908 on the foundation of the national Territorial Force (which became the Territorial Army in 1921). From 1914 it was the base of the 6th Battalion the Duke of Wellington's West Riding Regiment and, probably in 1936, it became the Scout Hall, a purpose it still serves. From c. 1971 to 1979 the hall was also where the Pentecostal congregation met.

The 'necessaries' on Kirkgate

In the days before universal flush toilets it was common practice in the nineteenth century for external facilities to be provided. In legal documents they were often euphemistically called 'necessaries' or the 'out-office'. At the lower end of the row on the north side of Kirkgate there is a small, double-door lean-to: this is the 'necessaries' mentioned in the 1844 tithe apportionment. [113]

Settle's pinfold

Almost every village or small town had a pinfold in the charge of the pinder; stray livestock were penned in the fold until redeemed, on payment of a fee imposed by the local manor court. In 1764 an agreement was made to pull down the existing pinfold just south of the *Golden Lion* and replace it with a new one 'on the waste' 'two and a half yards high with coping stones protruding six inches' at the rate of 1s. 4d. per square yard and at a total cost of £8 10s. [114] The new pinfold was renovated as a place to sit and rest and prior to that, in 1994, a tree was planted within it to commemorate the fortieth anniversary of the Yorkshire Dales National Park and the centenary of the Local Government Act which created the civil parish system. In the woods just above the pinfold was Settle Upper Reservoir, constructed in 1904-05, closed in the mid 1990s and finally drained in 2009.

The Poor House in Upper Settle, 1759-1834

Lettsom's map of 1761-65 (see page 19) named Commercial Street as Stepney Lane and Albert Hill disparagingly as Pauper Street. This was because the town Poor House lay near the apex of the two streets, roughly where Twisleton's Yard is now. It is known to have been in existence by at least 1739, according to an entry in the Town Meeting records: Ruth Armistead was paid 40s. for undertaking 'care of the Work-House' for the following year, while Thomas Newhouse was responsible for 'care of the maintenance and labour of the persons' therein, again for 40s. In 1759, however, it was moved across Pauper Lane into what had been John Kidd's farmhouse (date-stone KI I 1692). William and John Birkbeck, Thomas Salisbury, Peter Wilson Overend, Thomas Carr, Abraham Sutcliffe and Richard Foster, all 'principle landowners' in Settle, and others came together to arrange for Salisbury to lease to the other parties two dwellings, a barn and two gardens for twenty-one years at £4 per year with the aim of turning the properties into a 'convenient poor-house sufficient to hold all the poor belonging to the said township of Settle'. This building – referred to in the Meeting as a 'Hospital' could accommodate over twenty 'paupers'. In 1834 the system of large Union Workhouses came into being, each serving several parishes: Settle's was sited in Giggleswick making the Upper Settle poor-house redundant.

The Shambles dominates the north side of Market Place. Described by Pevsner as a 'remarkable building', [115] it has been misunderstood and wrongly dated. Reality is that it was built by Robert Charnley c. 1780 as a row of shops with single-storey cottages above and basements below. [116] It may have been built on the site of an earlier building, recorded in 1684. In 1887 the building was purchased by the Settle Market Building Co. Ltd and the cottages were partially demolished and reconfigured by adding the upper storey and removing the external north stairway in 1888-89.

Sutcliffe Building, School Hill

This imposing building has been known by two names – Parker Buildings and Sutcliffe Building. It bears a date-stone 'P SE 1841' – this refers to Stephen and Elizabeth Parker who lived at Lodge farm above old Anley: in 1851 he was listed as a substantial farmer and a lime burner. The tithe apportionment (1844) listed him as owner/occupier of the building on this plot. Also resident in Upper Settle in 1851 was John Parker, aged 36, carpenter and mason. Frustratingly, the building is not identifiable from the 1851 census returns. In 1871 it was listed as Parker Buildings composed of two dwellings and in 1891 four; uncorroborated evidence has suggested it was built c. 1870 by John Parker. It is possible that what Stephen and his wife erected in 1841 was rebuilt thirty years later by John as multiple dwellings in a speculative venture as a source of rental income. Certainly, looking at it externally from all four sides emphasises that it could not have been conceived as anything other than high-density housing provision. Its origins, however, are known: a legal document was drawn up in 1838, involving among others John Tatham, the Cheapside druggist, concerning a plot of land between 'Folly Yard' and the 'Independent Chapel' (Zion), a plot described as 'waste land in front of the chapel'. [117] The purpose of the agreement was to facilitate erection of the 'proposed Sutcliffe Building': so-called because the plot of land formerly belonged to Henry Sutcliffe.

The Folly in 1947 (courtesy Museum of North Craven Life)

Pevsner perceived the architecture of Grade I-listed The Folly as 'in many ways capricious and wilful'. It is certainly unusual, enigmatic and ambitious and its history befits its unusual name. [118] It was built for Richard Preston (c. 1643-96) in the late 1670s, a man who it has often been said was involved in the tanning business. There is no evidence of this. How he could afford to build such a grand house, given that he seems to have had an 'ordinary' beginning is a mystery; why he wanted such a massive property is equally puzzling. Documentary sources strongly point to his having been a solicitor in Settle –

perhaps a not very successful one. He died intestate relatively young and his probate inventory shows that on his death The Folly was full of clutter, the top floor seemingly had nothing in it, and there were no books or valuable items – all very peculiar for someone of his supposed status. He bore no sons and after his death the house was retained by his widow and daughters but, in 1703, it was partitioned among his three daughters. After 1712 it ceased to be seen as a house to be cherished and went through a whole series of uses: low-status tenements, farmhouse (the last tenant being William Bowskill who gave up the tenancy in 1901), joiners' workshops, fish and chip shop, refreshment rooms, antiques shop, furniture shop, bank, surgery. Even its name has been controversial. In Preston's probate inventory it was referred to as 'Newhouse', the Dawsons who owned it after his death preferred 'Settle Hall'. An Indenture from 1776 referred to it as 'Settle Hall alias Preston House'. [119] It now houses the Museum of North Craven Life.

A sketch of the tollbooth showing its relationship to the Shambles (Riley Collection)

Before the Town Hall was built, the eastern side of Market Place, indeed life in the manor, was dominated by the tollbooth. It housed the town gaol, was the base for the town night watchman, had a balcony upon which the town crier probably made his pronouncements, contained the town jury room and the official town market measures, and even had room for ground-floor shops.

The Town Hall, painted in 1838 by an unknown artist (courtesy Museum of North Craven Life)

George Webster of Kendal designed the Town Hall built in 1832 in Gothic Revival style. To make its construction possible £5500 was raised in £10 shares, an enormous achievement but one that speaks of the degree of community spirit still evident in Settle today. [120] Accommodation for the caretaker was provided in the basement and, at times, the rest of the building contained a market hall, news room, library, savings bank and meeting room. It was not just the Town Hall for Settle itself but for the whole of Settle Rural District before that was subsumed within Craven District Council (CDC), based in Skipton, in 1974. By 2006 it was realised that the building was sadly unsustainable, requiring major investment to bring it up to an acceptable standard of repair and increasingly being a drain on CDC resources. Various options were considered to keep it in public ownership but in 2011 the decision was made to sell it for commercial redevelopment as a mix of flats, retail and office space including an office for the Town Council.

Town Head House with Castleberg as the backdrop (© Horner Collection)

Town Head was a seventeenth-century farmhouse rebuilt by a member of the successful Bolland family c. 1770 (after buying it in 1763), and rebuilt again in 1875 as a large Victorian villa. In that guise the frontage was realigned and a broad sweeping drive was laid through a park-like landscape from Church Street, next to the entrance to the churchyard, now marked by a large beech tree and a stone gate pillar. In the early 1970s the house was demolished and the grounds were taken for the present Townhead housing development. One of Town Head House's claims to fame is that it was latterly the home of local archaeologist Tot Lord and his Pig Yard Club Museum.

In 1851 the Rev'd James Robinson bought the land which housed the old National School and part of the garden of the *Spread Eagle Inn* because, with his philanthropic mien, he wanted to provide the town with a purpose-built music hall. Thus was born Victoria Hall on Kirkgate, originally with a very different frontage from the present one, opened to the public in October 1853. It never closed allowing it to justifiably promote itself as the oldest continuously-running music hall in the whole country – never closed, though during the COVID-19 crisis from March 2020 public performances had to be suspended but the Hall then took on the all-important role of Settle Community Response Centre. Originally just called The Music Hall it became Victoria Hall in 1893. It was built by James Winskill, using stone from his quarry at Eldroth, to a design by Edward Paley who also designed Lancaster's cathedral. The Hall's trustees are – again justifiably – proud of the stage actdrop which presents a hand-painted view of Settle executed in 1882 by local man Edmund Handby as a copy of an 1822 painting by George Nicholson. Over its long life, Victoria Hall has put on 'variety' music hall entertainment, concerts, plays, lectures, public meetings and – from 1919-39 – cinema shows, first as The Picturedrome and latterly Kirkgate Cinema. It was gifted to Settle Rural District Council by the Robinson family in 1918 and has been a self-supporting registered charity since 1999. It was fully renovated in 2000 and re-opened in the following year.

Settle War Memorial in its original position (source: Settle War Memorial, Unveiling Ceremony Order of Service, courtesy of Barbara Middleton)

Not strictly speaking a building, Settle War Memorial was unveiled in a solemn service of remembrance on 6 December 1925. It was built by Brassingtons of Bridge End Mill and erected in the middle of the road junction there. Changing traffic volumes led to its being re-sited in its present position in 1971 though not without controversy: the memorial was originally set within a small enclosure surrounded by stone walling and cast-iron railings. When it was re-positioned neither walling nor railings were put back. At the time of writing, the latter still languish in a council shed at the former Craven Lime Works in Langcliffe.

* * *

A book such as this cannot draw to an end without looking at Castleberg, the great towering limestone outcrop that so dominates the town centre. Lettsom's map from the 1760s clearly showed four stone slabs on the town-facing slopes below the crag which 'Stones formerly put shewing the time of day', marked IX to XII (o'clock). As shadows cast by the summit advanced downslope through the day each numbered stone slab was highlighted. In 1760 Bishop Pococke wrote of stones placed on the lower (then not wooded) slope, as well as the bowling green on the flat area beyond the summit, but Tennant's journal of his visit here in 1773 made no mention of the stones suggesting that by then the sun-dial was no longer extant.

Part-way up the hill there is a vertical rock face and a large flat area – this had been quarried away to feed a lime kiln. In the late eighteenth century Settle's inhabitants brought a case to the manor court against the limeburner as they feared his work would bring the hill down on the town damaging their houses. The court found in favour of the limeburner on the grounds that even if the hill did collapse 'it would tumble not towards the town, but the direct or contrary way'! [121] Around 1800, the zigzag path to the summit was created. In 1830 Castleberg was sold by auction on a 99-year lease describing it as 'that Romantic and Picturesque plot … now set out and used as a pleasure ground'. It was purchased by the Bolland family of Town Head House, [122] sold on in 1902 to the prominent Dawson family of Langcliffe Hall and in 1967 passed to the county council. Under private ownership it had been a 'recreation ground' with planted flowers and shrubs, swings and hobby horse, roller skating and other pursuits. Adults were admitted on payment of 2d. with children at half price. [123] In 2019 ambitious plans were mooted, and funding sought, to restore Castleberg to its former glory for public use, spearheaded by the town council. In addition, twenty-six rock climbing routes have been created with grades ranging from f4** (easy) to f7a+** (hard).

Sources and Notes

Abbreviations

NCHT   North Craven Heritage Trust
NYCRO North Yorkshire County Record Office, Northallerton
WRRD   West Riding Registry of Deeds, Wakefield
WYAS   West Yorkshire Archive Service
YAHS   Yorkshire Archaeological and Historical Society
YDMT   Yorkshire Dales Millennium Trust
YDNPA Yorkshire Dales National Park Authority

Note All uses of the years 1851/61/71/81/91 and 1901 refer to census returns.

1. A very useful A4 leaflet – *GeoTrails. Ribblesdale Trail. Settle & Stainforth* – explains the geological situation in accessible language. It was published by the YDMT, YDNPA and the North Yorkshire Geological Partnership.
2. See T. Lord and J. Howard. 2013. 'Cave archaeology' in T. Waltham and D. Lowe (eds) *Caves and Karst of the Yorkshire Dales vol. 1.* Buxton: British Cave Research Association, pp. 239-51.
3. For an examination of Anglo-Saxon settlements and wider links in the Ingleborough area, see D.S. Johnson. 2019. *New Light on the "Dark Ages" in North Craven. Recent Advances in the Archaeology of the Yorkshire Dales.* Kettlewell: Yorkshire Dales Landscape Research Trust; Clapham: YDMT.
4. The National Archives, Calendar of Charter Rolls, C53.41.
5. https://discovery.nationalarchives.org.uk/details/r/C4294058. Thanks are due to Mike Slater for drawing this to my attention.
6. R.W. Hoyle (ed.) 1987. *Early Tudor Craven: Subsidies and Assessments 1510 – 1547.* Leeds: Yorkshire Archaeological Society, Record Series vol. CXLV.
7. YAHS, Clifford Family MSS, DD121/112/22, Court Rolls, Settle and Giggleswick, 'Court at *Clethop*' 22 October 1420 and 17 May 1421.
8. Devonshire Archives, Chatsworth, L/45/. Transcriptions available at https://www.dalescommunityarchives.org.uk.
9. T. Brayshaw and R.M. Robinson. 1932 *A History of the Ancient Parish of Giggleswick.* London: Halton & Co., p. 120.

10. T. Lord and M. Slater. 2019. 'The Settle market charters' *NCHT Journal*, pp. 24-27.

11. R. Pococke, Bishop of Neath and Ossory. 1888. *The Travels through England of Dr. Richard Pococke*. Edited by J.J. Cartwright, vol. 1. *Journey into England from Dublin*. Camden Society, New Series 42.

12. W. Roberts (ed.). 2001. *Thomas Gray's Journal of his Visit to the Lake District in October 1769*. Liverpool: Liverpool University Press.

13. T. Pennant. 1801. *A Tour from Downing to Alston-Moor*. London: Edward Harding, pp. 111-12. Downing Hall in Flintshire was the family seat.

14. E.W. Dayes. 1805, posthumously. *The Works of the Late Edward Dayes: containing an Excursion through the Principal Parts of Derbyshire and Yorkshire*. London: Mrs Dayes, pp. 56-62.

15. A. King. 2005. 'Settle and John Lettsom' *NCHT Journal*, pp. 17-19. Lettsom's parents had seven pairs of male twins: tragically, of the fourteen, John and his twin brother were the only ones to survive.

16. H. Whitbread (ed.). 2010. *The Secret Diaries of Miss Anne Lister (1791 – 1840)*. London: Virago, p. 389. I am grateful to Mary Slater for this link.

17. G.J. White. 2012. *The Medieval English Landscape 1000 – 1540*. London: Bloomsbury.

18. N. Millea. 2007. *The Gough Map. The Earliest Road Map of Great Britain?* Oxford: Bodleian Library.

19. WYAS, Wakefield, QD3/6.

20. John Ogilby. 1675. *Britannia*.

21. Quoted in Brayshaw and Robinson 1932, p. 161.

22. This line was shown clearly on Thomas Jefferys' *Map of Yorkshire* of 1771 which showed the roads bifurcating as described above.

23. The section of road alongside the Ribble is still marked on modern Ordnance Survey maps as an 'Other route with public access'.

24. Ordnance Survey 25 inch edition, sheet 132.6, surveyed in 1892.

25. 'An Act for repairing, amending, and widening, the Road from Keighley in the West Riding of the County of York, to Kirkby in Kendal in the County of Westmorland begun 10 November 1747 and carried on to 11 January 1753, Preamble', p. 3. Keighley Local Studies Library, BK354.

26. The Trust was wound up and the road 'disturnpiked' as responsibility for road maintenance passed from the Trusts to the Quarter Sessions and from 1888 to county councils.

27. Two of the 1760s mileposts survive as wall throughstones on the original turnpike road, Old Road, west of Clapham. They are very crudely inscribed: see D.S. Johnson. 2020. *Ingleborough. Landscape and History*. Revised edition. Lancaster: Carnegie.

28. J.J. Brigg. 1927. *The King's Highway in Craven being Notes on the History of the Yorkshire Portion of the Keighley and Kendal Turnpike Road.* Cross Hills: Dixon and Stell.

29. YAHS. MS 1186. 'Plan of a proposed canal from Parkfoot Bridge to Settle, 1780'; D.S. Johnson 2007. 'An overdose of optimism in the canal age: two abortive proposals in the Craven area of North Yorkshire'. *Industrial Heritage* 33 (1), pp. 33-41.

30. WYAS Wakefield, WYL 162, 1769; YAHS. MD335/1/10/6/15, 'Arguments against the Settle Navigation' 1774; Johnson 2007.

31. Brayshaw and Robinson 1932, pp. 184-85.

32. Enclosure Award, Settle Banks, High Scarr; and Scaleber, 1759. WRRD map vol. 3/27; NYCRO, ZXF, Enclosure Award, High Hill and Halstead Pastures, 1804.

33. WRRD, Indenture of Assignment BJ 090/122, 20 September 1768.

34. Edward Baines. 1822. *History, Directory and Gazetteer, of the County of York, vol. 1 the West Riding. Leeds: Leeds Mercury; Pigot's Directory of Yorkshire 1834. Manchester*: J. Pigot & Co.; 1851 national census returns. In contrast to these figures, the Craven Muster Roll of 1803 (ref. NYCROP9), which included all men aged 17 to 55, listed thirteen boot and shoe makers, thirty-seven textile workers, sixty-five engaged in other trades and crafts, seventeen shopkeepers, six involved in tanning, four innkeepers and twenty farmers, out of a total of 215 men in that age range.

35. WRRD, Indenture BF 449/639, 21 May 1767.

36. WRRD, Indenture CA 434/605, 17 October 1777; Indenture CB 299/470, 18 March 1778.

37. WRRD, GU 365/394, Memorial of Assignment, 27 May 1818. In 1861 John Tatham, aged 67, was described as 'grocer, chemist and druggist'. The first element of the name 'Cheapside' derives from the OE word *cēap* (pronounced 'cheap') meaning market or sale. A *cēapman* (chapman) was a pedlar; the modern word 'cheap' (ie not expensive) has the same derivation.

38. C. and G. Ball. 2015. 'The shop now known as Castleberg Outdoors, Cheapside, Settle'. *NCHT Journal*, pp. 14-15. An 'Italian warehouseman' sold groceries for the discerning customer – dried fruits, olive oil, pickles and exotic fruits.

39. V.E. Pitts. 1959. 'Story of the Craven Bank'. *Dalesman*, 21 (6), pp. 409-12.

40. Anon. n.d. *A Hundred Years of Settle Co-op 1861-1961.* Settle Co-operative Society.

41. WYAS, Bradford, 58D86/1/23/2, Settle Co-operative Society, Minute Book 1887-1899; 58D86/1/23/3, 1909-1911.

42. 58D86/1/23/8, 1937-40.
43. 58D86/1/23/9 and 10, 1940-1945 and 1949-1959.
44. 58D86/1/23/11, 1960-1968.
45. M. Slater. 2016. 'The Settle Gas supply, retorts and stumps' *NCHT Journal*, pp. 24-25; CM. Howarth. 2017. 'More about Settle gas works and stumps'. NCHT Journal, pp. 38-39.
46. Quoted in Brayshaw and Robinson 1932, pp. 41-42.
47. G.H. Brown. 1896. *On Foot around Settle*. Settle: J.W. Lambert, p. 143.
48. G. Ingle. 1997. *Yorkshire Cotton. The Yorkshire Cotton Industry, 1780 – 1835*. Lancaster: Carnegie Publishing.
49. Edward Baines. 1835. *History of the Cotton Manufacture in Great Britain*. London: Fisher, Fisher and Jackson, p. 387.
50. WRRD, CS 162/239, 1 April 1786, Assignment; CY 024/020, 18 July 1788, Assignment.
51. J. Nelson. 1994. 'The water mills of Ribblesdale'. *NCHT Journal*, pp. 17-19; Ingle, 1997, pp. 230-31.
52. WRRD, ED 601/816, 17 June 1800, Assignment.
53. G. Ingle. 2009. *Yorkshire Dales Textile Mills. A History of all the Textile Mills in the Yorkshire Dales from 1784 until the present Day*. Hebden Bridge: Royd Press, p. 134.
54. WRRD, CD 368/522, 26 August 1778, Assignment.
55. NYCRO, NCD/008/012, 13 December 1856, Indenture. An earlier indenture concerned John and Thomas Proctor of Runley Bridge, 'cotton spinners & calico manufacturers', and their involvement with a 'cotton mill near the corn mill called Settle Mill' (WRRD, JL 231/247, 8 September 1825, Memorial of Indenture).
56. WRRD, EH 687/845, 12 May 1801, Mortgage.
57. I am grateful to John Reid, an employee of the company from 1959-66, for his insights into Brassingtons.
58. N. Pevsner. 1967. *Yorkshire West Riding. The Buildings of England*. Harmondsworth: Penguin, p. 443.
59. I am grateful to the Priest-in-Charge at Holy Ascension, and to John Diggles, for this information. A perpetual curate was appointed by the bishop to officiate at a church which had neither vicar nor rector.
60. Brayshaw and Robinson, 1932, p. 98.
61. T. Whitehead. 1930. *History of the Dales Congregational Churches*. Keighley: Feather Bros.
62. Brown, 1896, p. 33.
63. A. Read. 2019. 'Zion Independent Congregational Chapel in Upper Settle'. *NCHT Journal*, pp. 28-31.

64. O.A. Beckerlegge. 1975. 'The evolution of the Settle Circuit'. *Proceedings of the Wesley Historical Society*, 40, pp. 34-44.
65. J. Woollerton, Rev'd. n.d. *A Souvenir Handbook of the Centenary of Settle Methodist Circuit* (1830-1930).
66. Beckerlegge, 1975, p. 36.
67. I am indebted to Sally Waterson of Settle Christian Fellowship for helping me with its history. Interestingly, in a sense Pentecostalism grew out of Primitive Methodism as many followers, like their Primitive forebears, eschewed Methodism's central control and direction and sought a purer and simpler form of worship.
68. Brown, 1896, p. 47.
69. R.G.K. Gudgeon. 1999. *A History of Catholic Life in the Settle, Giggleswick, Lawkland and surrounding Area*. Unpublished pamphlet.
70. An advertisement for a pupil teacher on such apprenticeship terms was posted in the *Settle Chronicle and North Ribblesdale Advertise*r, 1 June 1854.
71. WRRD, LM 434/367, 7 December 1807, Indenture.
72. WRRD, LM 446/376, 26 April 1834, Indenture.
73. R. Hudson. 2005. 'The rise and fall of a building – Settle Mechanics' Hall' *NCHT Journal*, 2005, pp. 24-26; S. Harrop. 2006. 'Settle Mechanics' Institute 1831-1887' *NCHT Journal*, pp. 18-22.
74. Thanks are due to Graeme Lawson for this snippet. He was 'in charge' of controlling passing traffic while the building was demolished.
75. *Settle Chronicle*, 1 June 1854.
76. Jean Asher. 2015. *The Story of the Settle Meeting House.*
77. G.H. Brown, 1896, pp. 48-49.
78. Anon. 2017. 'Marshfield House, Parents' National Educational Union (PNEU) Preparatory School in Settle' *NCHT Journal*, pp. 5-7; The National Archives, ED 172/448/3.
79. K. Kinder. 2019. 'Dr E Margaret Buckle, Dales poet and teacher at Settle Girls' High School', *NCHT Journal*, pp. 4-7.
80. D.S. Johnson. 2019. *Time Please! "Lost Inns, Pubs and Alehouses of the Yorkshire Dales*. Settle: NCHT. Much of this chapter is derived from this publication.
81. NYCRO, ZXF(M), 1/7/30, n.d.
82. West Riding Quarter Sessions records for 1771 and 1803; trade directories for 1822-1904.
83. WRRD, AC 454/342, 10 May 1749, Assignment; AC 455/342, 20 May 1749, Indenture. Between 1749 and 1760 the inn changed hands six times.
84. In Frederic Riley's 1933 *Guide to Settle. A Practical Handbook for the Visitor & Tourist.*

85. Borthwick Institute, vol. 91, fol. 372, 1747.
86. WRRD, LW 195-96/140, 8 May 1834, Memorial of Indenture; MC 013/013, 26 May 1835, Memorial of Indenture.
87. C. Bruyn Andrews (ed.). 1970. *The Torrington Diaries*, vol. 3. (first published 1936). New York: Barnes and Noble; London: Methuen; pp. 94-96.
88. WRRD, CF 231/287, 3 July 1779, Memorial of Indenture.
89. Borthwick Institute, vol. 91, 2 February 1736.
90. W. Howson. 1850. *An Illustrated Guide to the Curiosities of Craven*. London: Whittaker & Co; Settle: Wildman.
91. WRRD, MF 171/182, 20 November 1836, Memorial.
92. Borthwick Institute, Admin JC, 3 June 1743.
93. WRRD, IH 678-79/653, 27 and 28 June 1825; LC 610/544, 9 and 10 March 1832; LJ 83/89, 4 June 1832; LK 648/583, 29 and 30 April 1833;MO 595/615, 19 July 1837 – all Memorials of Indenture.
94. WRRD, JN 412/399, 12 and 13 January 1826, Memorial of Indenture.
95. WRRD, MA 575/535, 3 August 1835, Memorial of Indenture.
96. Brown, 1896, p. 50.
97. E.M.J. Miller (ed.). 1973. *An Appreciation of Settle*. Settle & District Civic Society, no pagination.
98. M.J. Slater. 2014. 'Rev. John Robinson and Alphonsine Sarah Jarry Charities'. *NCHT Journal*, pp. 3-4.
99. M. Slater. 2009. 'John Birkbeck (1817-1890) and John Birkbeck (1842-1892), mountaineers' *NCHT Journal*, pp. 16-17.
100. In summer 1985 this writer was asked to – temporarily – take on the role of 'looking after' Anley Estate for the Birkbecks. He stepped down from that role at the end of March ... 2017!
101. M. and M. Slater. 2017. 'Surgeons, apothecaries and man-midwives – Settle medics from the 17th to the 20th century' *NCHT Journal*, pp. 8-12.
102. D. Johnson. 2010. *Limestone Industries of the Yorkshire Dales*. Stroud: Amberley, pp. 148-65.
103. D.S. Johnson. 2005. *Foredale Quarry, Ribblesdale Limeworks,Helwith Bridge, North Yorkshire. An Industrial Archaeology Survey of the Quarry*. Settle: Hudson History, pp. 7-8.
104. M. and M. Slater, 2017.
105. Brayshaw and Robinson, 1932, p. 174.
106. The Craven Herald, 30 May 1890.
107. Patent no. 2495 of 1872, patent no. 4286 of 1889; Johnson, 2010, pp. 73-75.
108. Pevsner, 1967, p. 443.
109. See, for example, WRRD, LS/639/632, 13 August 1834 and MF 171/182, 20 November 1836, both Memorials of Indenture.

110. J. Stansfeld. 1885. *History of the Family of Stansfeld of Stansfield in the Parish of Halifax*. Leeds: Goodall & Suddick.

111. G.R .Kelly. (ed.) 1877. *The Post Office Directory of the West Riding of Yorkshire*. London: Kelly & Co., pp. 195-97, 200-01.

112. Brayshaw and Robinson, 1932, p. 175.

113. A Memorial of Indenture, 3 April 1821, concerned various properties in Duke Street including the 'Necessary house', WRRD, HL 237/223; another, dated 13 August 1834, referred to the *New Inn* and its ancillary buildings which included 'Outoffices', WRRD, LS 639/632.

114. YAHS, MD435, 1764, 'Settle pinfold, agreement'; Brayshaw and Robinson, 1932, p. 175.

115. Pevsner, 1967, p. 443; the word Shambles derives from the Old English word *scamol* meaning a stool or vending bench and the Latin *scamnum* which had the same meanings – 'sc' in Old English was pronounced like the modern English 'sh'. By the 1540s the word shambles referred to a place where meat was sold.

116. T.H. Foxcroft. 1997. 'The Settle Market Buildings Co. Ltd' *NCHT Journal*, p. 21; R.W. Hoyle. 2014. 'The Shambles in Settle Marketplace (sic), its date and builder' *Yorkshire Archaeological Journal* 86, pp. 228-36.

117. WRRD, MY 499/475, 29 May 1838, Indenture.

118. A. Read. 2009. 'In praise of the Folly: past, present and future' *NCHT Journal*, pp. 8-10; R. Hoyle. 2011. *The Identity of Richard Preston*. http://www.ncbpt.org.uk/folly/; P. Brears and R. Hoyle. 2018. *The Folly. Settle's House of Mystery*, Settle: North Craven Building Preservation Trust.

119. WRRD, BZ 312/419, 27 September 1776, Indenture of Assignment.

120. The final chapters of this book were written during the early days of the COVID-19 lockdown when Settle did itself proud.

121. J. Hutton. 1781. *A Tour to the Caves in the Environs of Ingleborough and Settle*, London: Richardson and Urquhart, p. 49.

122. WRRD, KW 281/274, 1/2 July 1830, Memorial of Indenture.

123. Information from Settle Town Council.

Further Reading

The reader who wishes to delve deeper into Settle's rich history will find the following useful.

Brayshaw, T. and Robinson, R.M. 1932. *A History of the Ancient Parish of Giggleswick*. London: Halton & Co.

P. and R. Hudson. 2000. *Take a closer Look at Settle. Four Town Walks.* Settle: Hudson History.

Since 1992 the NCHT has published an annual *Journal* with a focus on North Craven, the area within which Settle lies. Its contents are freely accessible at www.northcravenheritage.org.uk/NCHT/Journal_Index.

Giggleswick deserves its own volume so is not included in this book. A website dedicated to the parish was being developed at the time of writing, and can be accessed at www.stalkeldaschurchgiggleswick.org.uk.

Stories in Stone facilitated and funded, through the National Lottery Heritage Fund, a comprehensive online collation of local archival material, accessible at https://www.dalescommunityarchives.org.uk. Sheila Gordon transcribed hundreds of deeds from the WRRD which are all posted on this website.

Place-names

Modern name	Early name	Etymology	Meaning
Anley	Anele, Anlei	OE *ān, lēah*	lonely clearing
Attermire	Authulvesmire	ON *Auđulfr*, ON *mýrr*	Authulf's marsh
Butch Lane	Butts Lane	OE *butte*	(lane) abutting plough strips
Cammock	Cambok	Brit *cambok, āco*	crooked one
Cleatop	Clethop	OWSc *kléttr*, OE *hop*	small valley near a cliff
Halsteads	Allestodes	OE *hall stede*	site of a hall
Hunter Bark		OE *huntere, beorg*	hunter hill
Ingfield		OE *eng, feld*	water meadows
Mearbeck	Mearbecke	OE *mǽre*, ON *bekkr*	boundary stream
Runley	Rennelith	OE *renn, hliđ*	house on a slope
Scaleber	Skalebergh	OWSc *skáli*, OE *beorg*	hill with a shieling
Settle	Setel	OE *setel*	place, dwelling
Stockdale	Stocadale	OE *stoc, dæl*	valley with an outlying farm
Stubbing	Stubbinge	OE *stubbing*	clearing
Warrendale Knotts	Wardale Knots	OE *wareine, dæl, cnotta*	valley with hills and a warrren